T0339309

"The Trinity is the foundational doctrine of the Christian faith, but often Christians are not equipped to speak accurately about this doctrine or to articulate why it matters for discipleship. In this book, Brandon Smith provides a reliable and accessible pathway into the meaning and spiritual implications of trinitarian theology. He skillfully combines scriptural exegesis and broader theological reflection to show Bible readers where to go and what to watch out for when contemplating God as Father, Son, and Spirit. This is a welcome resource for everyone seeking to grow in the love and knowledge of our triune God."

—Steven J. Duby,
associate professor of theology, Phoenix Seminary

"If Jesus Christ is the treasure hidden in the field of the Scriptures, then *The Biblical Trinity* is a treasure map produced by the hand of a master cartographer. Brandon Smith's book shows readers how to find Jesus Christ in the Scriptures and, in finding him, how to treasure him as the Father's Spirit-anointed Son, our Maker, Redeemer, and Reward. I am delighted to see *The Biblical Trinity* in print and fully expect that it will make many readers rich."

—Scott R. Swain,
president, Reformed Theological Seminary, Orlando, FL

"For many Christians, it is hard to relate the technical terms and concepts involved in the doctrine of the Trinity to the more concrete language of Scripture. We often worry about making an artificial connection or feel intimidated at using the wrong language. By working through a series of key biblical passages through a Trinitarian lens, Brandon Smith helps us understand how the Trinity is ultimately not an obstacle, but an aid, in understanding Scripture. More than that, he offers a model of doing theology in a way that is doctrinally careful, historically informed, and devotionally edifying. I highly recommend this helpful, accessible book, which will help Christians discern in fresh ways the outline of the Father, the Son, and the Holy Spirit in the pages of the Bible."

—Gavin Ortlund,
senior pastor, First Baptist Church, Ojai, CA

"A refreshingly simple and yet profound book, Brandon Smith has invited readers who trust Scripture to trust the deep logic of its divine triune author. *The Biblical Trinity* is grounded in careful readings of biblical passages and then flowers in the major doctrines of the orthodox church. Anyone who desires to attend to the identity of God as revealed in Scripture will benefit from this book."

—Amy Peeler,
associate professor of New Testament,
Wheaton College

"It takes a trained ear to hear the Trinitarian rhythm of Scripture. Brandon Smith shares this gift, acquired at the feet of the Church Fathers, with those willing to learn how to listen for the one voice of the Father, Son, and Spirit. This is an eminently usable guide and introduction to the biblical foundations for the doctrine of the Trinity."

—Adonis Vidu,
Andrew Mutch Distinguished Professor of Theology,
Gordon-Conwell Theological Seminary

"Brandon Smith offers readers a terrific overview of the biblical doctrine of the Trinity. If you were to read just one chapter every day, perhaps after your daily Bible reading, within two weeks you will have encountered an overview of major Trinitarian passages in the Bible along with guidance on how to read the rest of the Bible in a Trinitarian manner. This worshipful and biblical explanation of the Trinity is a real gift to the church."

—Trevin Wax,
vice president of research and resource development,
North American Mission Board

"Christians are baptized in the name of the Trinity: Father, Son, and Holy Spirit. The confession of the Trinitarian faith is the deepest bond that all Christians share. Brandon Smith, in this short work, has given us a precise and compelling depiction of the unity of the Trinitarian faith and the practice of the Christian life of prayer. He depicts confessional truth claims and Christian devotion in unity with one another in a way that is compelling and can be of benefit to many. A very helpful book for Christian formation!"

—Thomas Joseph White,
OP, rector, Angelicum

The Biblical Trinity

ENCOUNTERING THE FATHER, SON, AND HOLY SPIRIT IN SCRIPTURE

The Biblical Trinity

ENCOUNTERING THE FATHER,
SON, AND HOLY SPIRIT
IN SCRIPTURE

BRANDON D. SMITH

LEXHAM PRESS

Print ISBN 9781683596974
Digital ISBN 9781683596981
Library of Congress Control Number 2022947469

Lexham Editorial: Todd Hains, Allisyn Ma, Cindy Huelat, Mandi Newell
Cover Design: Lydia Dahl, Brittany Schrock
Typesetting: Justin Marr

To Christa, Harper, Emma, and Amelia

The grace of the Lord Jesus Christ
and the love of God
and the fellowship of the Holy Spirit
be with you all.
—2 Corinthians 13:14 (ESV)

Contents

CHAPTER ONE
The Biblical Trinity 1

CHAPTER TWO
Forgiveness of Sins 13

CHAPTER THREE
Triune Commission 21

CHAPTER FOUR
The Word Made Flesh 31

CHAPTER FIVE
The Father and Son Give Life 43

CHAPTER SIX
I AM 51

CHAPTER SEVEN
The Comforter 61

CHAPTER EIGHT
Resurrection and Adoption 71

CHAPTER NINE
   The Mind of God 81

CHAPTER TEN
   A New Shema 89

CHAPTER ELEVEN
   The Ministry of the Spirit 95

CHAPTER TWELVE
   Triune Salvation 105

CHAPTER THIRTEEN
   Equality with God 115

CHAPTER FOURTEEN
   The Firstborn Image 123

CHAPTER FIFTEEN
   The Exact Imprint of His Nature 135

CHAPTER SIXTEEN
   Triune Worship 145

CHAPTER SEVENTEEN
   Three Rules for Reading Trinitarianly . . 157

Acknowledgments   165
Recommended Reading   167
Works Cited   169
Endnotes   173
Scripture Index   177

CHAPTER ONE

The Biblical Trinity

The Bible is a Trinitarian book. This statement may surprise you. After all, the word "Trinity" is found nowhere in the Bible. And if we are people of the Book, how can we describe the Bible this way if the doctrine is not even explicitly named in the pages of Scripture?

Doctrine is not a mere list or collection of the Bible's words; rather, doctrine is a type of speech about God, which at times requires drawing together a set of themes and patterns across the scope of the biblical canon. So, seeing the doctrine of the Trinity will require more than mere proof texts or word studies—it will require following the logic and grammar of Scripture.[1]

Jesus modeled this for us when he was tempted by Satan in the wilderness (Matt 4:1–11). They both used biblical citations in their arguments, but the difference was their usage of the texts. The way Satan used Scripture bent it to his interpretation, whereas Jesus's application held true to the context of Scripture. Satan quoted God's words—as he did in the garden of Eden—but misused them. Jesus, on the other hand, quoted Scripture correctly. For example, when Satan quoted Psalm 91 to tempt Jesus to jump off the temple, Jesus responded with Deuteronomy 6:16: "Do not test the Lord your God." Jesus pointed out clearly that Satan was misusing Psalm 91 because Satan wasn't quoting it in light of passages like Deuteronomy 6:16. Martin Luther summarizes this idea well: Satan and his demons "even while they speak truly according to grammar, that is, with respect to the words, they speak lies according to theology, that is, with respect to the sense."[2]

The goal of this book is to briefly show you how to see the Trinity in the Bible by introducing basic reading strategies and then modeling them in a select group of passages. Before we get to the biblical passages, we should ask two questions: (1) what is the Trinity?, and (2) how do we see the Trinity in the Bible?

WHAT IS THE TRINITY?

The doctrine of the Trinity seeks to explain the biblical data about who God is. As the biblical story unfolds, we see that God is *one being* (Deut 6:4). That said, the Bible also affirms that God is somehow *three persons*—Father, Son, and Holy Spirit. As we will see throughout this book, to speak of the one God of the Bible is to speak of the Father, Son, and Spirit—they are each God, but they are not each other.[3] Four basic theological principles can help us think about Scripture's revelation of our triune God.[4]

1. *Nature.* The Father is God, the Son is God, and the Holy Spirit is God. They are equal in nature because each is fully God. There is no hierarchy within the divine nature, such that the Son might be less divine than the Father, and so on. God cannot be something other than God, so the three persons have the same exact eternal existence, perfection, self-sufficiency, power, authority, knowledge, wisdom, and will because each person is fully God.

2. *Relations.* Again, the Father, Son, and Holy Spirit are each God, but they are not each other. They are each fully God, not three parts of God's one nature divided among them. But while there is no distinction in their nature as the one God, the primary distinction in the life of the triune God is the distinction between these three

persons and their relations to one another. We see this clearly in the way the Bible describes them. The Son is the "only begotten Son" of the Father (John 3:16). The Father, however, is unbegotten—the Bible never describes him as the Son of some other Father. The Holy Spirit proceeds from the Father and Son (John 14:26; 15:26), not the other way around. Each person, then, has a distinct relation to the others even as we rigorously affirm that they are the one God.

3. Inseparable operations. This principle of unity and distinction is most clearly shown in the undivided external acts of the triune God in creation and salvation. When one person of the Trinity acts, it is an indivisible act between all three. Because the Son and Holy Spirit are sent from the Father in salvation—primarily the Son becoming incarnate and the Holy Spirit being poured out at Pentecost—the personal distinctions are still maintained. For example, the Father doesn't put on flesh and dwell among us; the Son does. The doctrine of inseparable operations offers a category to talk about how Father, Son, and Holy Spirit always act with one divine power, authority, and will. The Father, Son, and Holy Spirit are distinct persons but not divided persons. Salvation, for instance, is the work of the one God, and that one God acts distinctly and yet inseparably as Father, Son, and Holy Spirit. And even when a biblical passage might only emphasize one or two persons acting, this doesn't mean that the unnamed person of the Trinity is off taking a heavenly nap. Instead, we understand the biblical affirmation that God is never divided or separated, and thus the persons always act indivisibly.

4. *The hypostatic union.* When doing Trinitarian theology, we also have to deal with the mystery of the incarnation of the Son. The Son has existed eternally as God, yet he "became flesh and dwelt among us" in time and space (John 1:14). He never ceased to be God, and yet became a man. As such, we affirm the hypostatic union: Christ is one divine person with two natures, fully God and fully man. He forgives sins with divine authority and yet bled and died for our sins as a perfect sacrifice; he created all things and sustains the universe with divine power, yet he also napped and ate; he existed before time began, and yet he walked the streets of Israel in the first century. The eternal Son—*that same person*—assumed a true human nature to live the perfectly obedient, sinless life that no mere human could. This mystery cannot be resolved or comprehended—it can only be affirmed based on the biblical witness.

These Trinitarian principles are derived from Scripture's depiction of our triune God. They serve as a grammar that shapes our speech and helps us speak rightly about God. Ultimately, we must confess that the Trinity is a revealed mystery. It is *revealed* in that the triune

God has revealed himself in three persons clearly in the Bible; it is not fully comprehensible in that we only "know in part" the mysteries of God (1 Cor 13:12). So, we should take confidence in the fact that God has revealed himself in a meaningful way, but the mystery should humble us before our mighty God. The question before us is how to see our triune God as he is revealed in Scripture.

HOW DO WE SEE THE TRINITY IN THE BIBLE?

The Bible teaches the doctrine of the Trinity in terms of language and logic, not merely proof texts or word studies. So, how do we read the Bible in order to see the truth and beauty of our triune God? In the following chapters, we will encounter a wonderful adventure of knowing and worshiping our triune God as he is revealed in the pages of Scripture. To do that, we will operate from two basic assumptions.

1. *The doctrine of the Trinity is rooted in the biblical story line.* The reason we even address a "Trinitarian" description of God is because Christ and the Spirit were sent to us. This is not to say that God has changed or that the Trinity is absent from the pages of the Old Testament. On the contrary, we see God's Word and Spirit at work in the Old Testament (for example, Gen 1:1–3; Ps 110; see also John 1:1; Heb 1:13). Jesus himself says that the Old Testament speaks of him (Luke 24:44; John 5:46).

Joel 2:28 was fulfilled in the Spirit's outpouring in Acts 2. Nonetheless, from a historical perspective, the Son's incarnation and the Spirit's outpouring in real time and space caused the earliest Christians to reconsider what it meant to believe in and worship the one God of Israel. Since titles, actions, and claims about Jesus and the Spirit were descriptions reserved for God himself, the earliest Christians were forced to examine what it meant to affirm, for example, Deuteronomy 6:4: "The LORD our God, the LORD is *one*."

We cannot rightly understand the New Testament without the Old Testament, for the New Testament authors' claims about Jesus and the Spirit are rooted in their confession of the Old Testament's authority. God's providential ordering of human history meant that the Old Testament was already a witness to Christ and the Spirit long before the New Testament was written because (1) the Old Testament was always pointing forward; and (2) Jesus's and the Spirit's self-identification with the identity and purposes of God himself became the biblical authors' interpretive grid for the fulfillment of such expectations.[5] And since there is a strict distinction between the creator and his creatures/creation, the three persons of the Trinity sit alone in eternal divine blessedness on the creator's side of creation. In turn, we cannot fully understand Scripture without considering how its representation of God's nature and purposes relate to the persons and works of Christ and the Spirit. Every New Testament passage covered in this book, then, is rightly understood in light of its own claims and its relationship to Old Testament texts and themes. When we read the whole Bible, we are pressured by its claims to confess a triune God.

2. *The doctrine of the Trinity was received by the Christian tradition as a faithful reading of Scripture's presentation of God.* This, too, is rooted in the providence of God. Just as the New Testament authors did not create some Trinitarian doctrine that was foreign to the Old Testament, the post-apostolic church was and is guided by the Spirit to understand and apply the biblical canon's witness to God in their own time and space. For the majority of church history, there has been a general agreement with the rule of faith, which taught that Scripture is an interconnected story that reveals a true picture of the Father, Son, and Spirit—the foundation of our faith.[6] So, if we deny the Trinity, not only would we be overlooking Scripture's own depiction of God, but we would be abandoning two millennia of faithful Christian readers before us.

In sum, we read Scripture in a theological-canonical way with the triune God as our subject matter. We read *theologically* because Scripture is inspired by and points to the triune God. We read *canonically* because we understand Scripture—Old Testament and New Testament—as a unified story or message about the triune God. These assumptions will guide us as we consider a handful of texts that help us see the Trinity in the Bible.

I have chosen passages that offer some of the clearest examples of the doctrine of the Trinity. Some texts are focused on the interactions of all three persons, and others may focus primarily on the Son or Spirit, but all help build a full-fledged biblical doctrine of the Trinity. These texts and many others are not in competition with one another. It's not as though some are more "Trinitarian" than others. Instead, what we find is a choir of voices across the biblical canon that sing a beautiful song about our triune God. It's my ultimate hope that this book sparks or renews your love for our triune God and his Scriptures, that you may hear his song as you read its pages. Though in many ways the Trinity is a mystery to us, nonetheless God has meaningfully revealed himself to us in Scripture in this way.

May we spend the rest of our days seeking to know and glorify this triune God. May we continue to seek his grace and mercy as we seek to offer our lives to him as living sacrifices.

A PRAYER

O God the Father, Creator of heaven and earth,
    Have mercy upon us.
    O God the Son, Redeemer of the world,
    Have mercy upon us.
    O God the Holy Ghost, Sanctifier of the faithful,
    Have mercy upon us.
    O holy, blessed, and glorious Trinity, one God,
    Have mercy upon us.[7]

CHAPTER TWO

Forgiveness of Sins
MATTHEW 9:1-8

I n our home, we have an informal catechism that we often use with our daughters. It goes like this:

> I ask, "Can you forgive your own sins?"
>> My daughters reply, "No!"
> "Can daddy forgive your sins?"
>> "No!"
> "Can mommy forgive your sins?"
>> "No!"
> "What about your baby sister? She's cute and cuddly and sweet."
>> "No!"
> "Who alone can forgive your sins?"
>> "God!"

They know only God can forgive their sins—they have been taught this for as long as they can remember. God's people were catechized the same way. Psalm 3:8 says plainly, "Salvation belongs to the LORD." And biblically speaking, God's salvation has physical and spiritual effects, because sin has both physical and spiritual effects.

We can think of the sacrificial system, in which God forgives his people's sins through sacrifices. We can think of God leading the Israelites out of Egypt or providing manna and water in the wilderness. In Isaiah, God says both "I am the one, I sweep away your transgressions for my own sake and remember your sins no more" (Isa 43:25) and "I will create new heavens and a new earth" (Isa 65:17). In whatever way it happens, it's God alone who saves and it's his prerogative to save.

Now, imagine for a moment that you're a devout Jewish person who hears Jesus claim that *he* can forgive sins. If someone walked up to you today and said, "I can forgive your sins," you would be confused and perhaps even offended. In Matthew 9, Jesus claims to forgive sins and is called a blasphemer—one who speaks profanely about God. Why? Because the Jewish leaders knew that his claim to be able to forgive sins was something that the Hebrew Scriptures attributed to God alone.

SINS FORGIVEN AND CREATION RESTORED

Blasphemy! The religious leaders hurl this insult at Jesus numerous times in the New Testament. In fact, we will see this word come up a few times in subsequent chapters of this book. To call someone a blasphemer is to call him the worst of sinners. And the Jewish leaders accuse Jesus of blasphemy because they recognize that he is very clearly claiming to be God. If he isn't God, then they're right. But if he is, they've missed the offer of salvation that (literally) stands in front of them.

Matthew 9 opens as a group of men lead Jesus to a paralyzed man. This man has been hopeless, resigned to a life on his back. The stretcher he lies on is the stretcher he may die on. With the growing reputation of Jesus's miraculous deeds, Jesus seems to be the paralyzed man's last hope. And he was right. Jesus not only planned to deal with his physical ailment, but also his spiritual ailment. Jesus tells the man that his sins are forgiven.

This troubles Jewish leaders. "Blasphemy," they say to themselves. After all, who can forgive sins but God? And yet this man is claiming to do something only God can do. If this paralyzed man has sinned, then he should seek forgiveness from God alone. Perhaps he should go the temple like everyone else, rather than being laid out in someone's living room. But his sins are forgiven right then and there merely because Jesus, God in the flesh, spoke the words.

After the leaders inwardly utter "blasphemy," the passage says that Jesus "perceives their thoughts," which sounds similar to Jeremiah 17:10: "I, the LORD, examine the mind, I test the heart." Not only does he have the authority to forgive sins, but he also exercises a deep, even divine, knowledge of their innermost thoughts. Jesus doesn't back down after being accused of blasphemy; instead, he doubles down:

> Which is easier: to say, "Your sins are forgiven," or to say, "Get up and walk"? But so that you may know that the Son of Man has authority on earth to forgive sins"—then he told the paralytic, "Get up, take your stretcher, and go home." So he got up and went home. When the crowds saw this, they were awestruck and gave glory to God, who had given such authority to men. (Matt 9:5–8)

Jesus challenges their suspicion. It might be easy for someone to merely say, "Your sins are forgiven." You or I could say something like that, and there would be no real proof. So Jesus ups the ante and tells the man to get up and walk. Why? "So that you may know that the Son of Man has authority on earth to forgive sins." Jesus doesn't back down here; no, he ensures that the charge of blasphemy is proven false. God has promised from the beginning not only to cleanse our spiritual death, but to redeem all of creation. The total redemption of this man—body and soul—was the proof.

While some in the crowd may have seen Jesus as merely an amazing man, the religious leaders knew his claim was bigger. When Jesus forgives the man's sins *and* tells him to get up and walk, he is claiming and demonstrating that he is God himself, with the power and prerogative to "sweep away their sins" (Isa 43:19) as well as "make all things new" (Isa 44:22). A mere man could not do this. Prophets, priests, judges, and kings were held in esteem among God's people. They were messengers and witnesses to the promises of God. Their offices were appointed by God and used by God in innumerable ways. But as Jesus said, these righteous people longed for his coming (Matt 13:17; John 8:56). They were all imperfect. People at the center of biblical covenants—like Noah, Abraham, and David—were all sinners with obvious flaws. But nobody assumed that these people were God, nor did these people ever claim to be. They were mere signposts on the way to the Messiah's arrival.

After four hundred years, John the Baptist's voice cried out in the wilderness—a voice promised in Isaiah 40—saying, "Repent, because the kingdom of heaven has come near! ... Prepare the way for the LORD" (Matt 3:1, 3; see also Mark 1:2–5; Luke 3:2–6; John 1:23). This Lord—Jesus Christ, God in the flesh—was coming to save his people from their sins and bear their punishment on his own shoulders. During his earthly ministry, people began to see his reconciling work with their own eyes. Jesus shows the religious leaders that God himself has finally come; the only one who can forgive sins stepped into creation to redeem it from the inside out.

TOWARD A RENEWAL OF ALL THINGS

This passage focuses primarily on Jesus's divinity, as the person of the Trinity who became man for our sake. The Father, Son, and Holy Spirit are each fully God, but only the person of the Son put on flesh and dwelt among us as the God-man, Jesus Christ. Nonetheless, it is the triune God who makes all things new, which is evident in the context of this passage. The Father and Holy Spirit's unified work in the ministry of Jesus is clear throughout the Gospel, so we should not assume that because the other persons of the Trinity are not listed in this particular passage, that they are absent or taking a break. Indeed, the New Testament consistently portrays Jesus's miraculous works as inseparable from the Holy Spirit's work (for example, Mark 3:28–30).

Jesus's work on earth is the interpretive grid through which the earliest Christians understood the inbreaking of God's kingdom and his plan to deliver them from sin and death. Some people accepted this claim. Others, like the leaders in this passage, thought this claim was flat-out sinful. When Jesus claimed to forgive sins, his audience then, and now, are faced with C. S. Lewis's famous question: Is Jesus a liar, lunatic, or Lord?[8]

If he really is able to forgive sins, then God's promises really do find their "amen" and "yes" in him (2 Cor 1:20), because he is the God who made the promise and who keeps his promises. In fact, only *God* can keep God's promises. If he is not God in the flesh, then God's promise to deliver us and all of creation from the curse of sin is still a mystery. More than that, the religious leaders would be right: he is a blasphemer and a liar or lunatic of the evilest sort. A truly biblical understanding of the forgiveness of sins requires the doctrine of the Trinity—Jesus must be the eternal, divine Son of God in order to have the power and authority to forgive sins and redeem all things.

A PRAYER

Father, you sent your only begotten Son for us and for our salvation. By your Spirit grant that we would receive Jesus's words, "Your sins are forgiven." In Jesus's name, by the Spirit we pray. Amen.

CHAPTER THREE

Triune Commission
MATTHEW 28:18-20

We have friends who are particularly thoughtful about how they name their children. Each child's name has a deep meaning that their parents hope sets a trajectory for their whole lives. When one looks through biblical names, they are often filled with meaning. For example, Joshua means "God's deliverance," and he was, indeed, the deliverer of God's people to the promised land. My wife and I, on the other hand, chose our girls' names because we thought they were classic, beautiful girls' names. When our oldest, Harper, asked us what her name means, she was a little disappointed to find out that it simply means "harp player."

Though we placed a relatively low priority on the meaning of our children's names, God's name is at the core of his self-revelation. At Sinai, he told Moses that he should be called "I AM WHO I AM," revealing his eternal nature and unmatched glory and power (Exod 3:14). From the start, God wanted his image-bearers taking his name to every inch of the globe (Gen 1:26–28). And in the baptismal formula of the Great Commission, the church is given the same call as Adam and Eve and all of God's people to take God's triune name and image to the ends of the earth.

BAPTISM AND THE GREAT COMMISSION

In the Great Commission, we are marked with God's name at our baptism:

> Jesus came near and said to them, "All authority has been given to me in heaven and on earth. Go, therefore, and make disciples of all nations, baptizing them in the name of the Father and of the Son and of the Holy Spirit, teaching them to observe everything I have commanded you. And remember, I am with you always, to the end of the age." (Matt 28:18–20)

We are baptized into the one name of the triune God. In this formula, we see the Trinity in both singular and plural terms—one God, three persons. The commission to go to the ends of the earth carries with it the command and authority of God himself. Of course, we do not make disciples or baptize in our own names; we also do not make disciples in the name of Jesus alone. Instead, our triune God calls, equips, and sends us into his mission to reconcile all things to himself. This commission is not unique to the New Testament—God delegated authority to his people to bear his name all the way back in the garden of Eden.

Years before Jesus gives this final triune commission, his own baptism was a Trinitarian act and perhaps the pivotal jumpstart to his public ministry:[9]

> When Jesus was baptized, he went up immediately from the water. The heavens suddenly opened for him, and he saw the Spirit of God descending like a dove and coming down on him. And a voice from heaven said, "This is my beloved Son, with whom I am well-pleased." (Matt 3:16–17)

God the Son was sent into the world (John 3:16) as the second Adam (Rom 5:12–21) to redeem mankind. Because no human could live a perfect, sinless life, God himself took on flesh and dwelt among us (John 1:1–18). This is reinforced by his baptism. One might ask, "Why would God need to be baptized?" In fact, this was essentially

John the Baptist's question (Matt 3:14). Jesus's answer—"to fulfill all righteousness"—shows that his mission on earth was to relive the human story perfectly and obediently. His perfection would become our perfection.

This was God's plan all along: to redeem his people and continue his mission of filling the earth with image-bearers. Jesus's baptism shows us the unity and distinction of the Trinitarian persons quite obviously. The Father speaks from heaven, the Son is in the water, and the Spirit comes down in the appearance of a dove.

As we have already seen, it is the triune God who saves. Jesus is not out on an island doing clean-up work for the Father; no, the Father, Son, and Spirit act inseparably in God's mission. On the one hand, we see a picture of our triune God's unity: the Father sending the Son, the Son becoming a man and thus becoming obedient to the Father according to his humanity, and the Spirit being poured out. We see the triune God speaking and acting in one accord. On the other hand, we see that the Father is not in the water, the Son does not come down from heaven in this moment, and so on.

The triune God's mission of his name and image being spread to the ends of the earth continues and is ramped up here at Jesus's baptism. It is a clear introductory picture that the Father, Son, and Spirit are equally integral to God's mission in the world. To talk about God's name and mission is to talk about the Trinity's name and mission. Here in the water, we see heaven and earth brought together both in the person of Jesus and the Spirit's descent.

Jumping forward once again to the Great Commission, we see that Jesus called his disciples to baptize more disciples in the *one* name of the *three* persons. His baptism acts as a figure of this: the three persons present at the one baptism—unity in distinction. This is not a contradiction, but rather the way the text pressures us to make sense of God's unity and distinction.[10]

Going back to the garden of Eden, the mission of our triune God is founded on and rests in his power and authority. So when Jesus says to his disciples, "All authority on heaven and earth has been given to me," he is making clear that his authority—the authority of God himself—is delegated to us as we go about being fruitful and multiplying disciples in his name on his mission. The Son with whom the Father is well-pleased is the Son who is well-pleased to send his disciples to the ends of the earth.

There is true power in God's name. It is not a mere title or designation. As we mentioned above, his name reflects his eternal nature and glory and power. This power upholds the expanse of the universe and even the cells that hold your body together. All of heaven confirms this right now, as you read this book, shouting with one voice, "Our Lord and God, you are worthy to receive glory and honor and power, because you have created all things, and by your will they exist and were created" (Rev 4:11).

The name is comprised of the Father, Son, and Spirit: the Father, who bestows all good gifts on his people, most notably the gifts of his Son and Spirit; the Son, who put on flesh and dwelt among us, living a perfectly obedient human life, dying a true death, raising bodily from the dead, and ascending to the right hand of the Father in the power and glory he shared with the Father before the foundation of the world (John 17:5); the Spirit, sent so that God's people will be "clothed with power from on high" (Luke 24:49 ESV)—the mediated power of God himself.[11] Thus, our involvement in the Great Commission is nothing more than obedience to the triune God's mission with the power of the triune God's name.

JOINING THE MISSION

In the early church, Jesus's baptism and the baptismal formula in the Great Commission were complementary portraits of the Trinity and its importance for our salvation. Augustine of Hippo said that Jesus's baptism is one of the clearest teachings on the Trinity,[12] and Hilary of Poitiers noted the same about the Great Commission. While many believe that the Trinity is the most difficult doctrine of Scripture, Augustine and Hilary noted its clarity in these passages. As Hilary said of this baptismal Trinitarian language, "What is there pertaining to the mystery of man's salvation that it does not contain?"[13] Augustine and Hilary's reasoning was rather simple: in these biblical scenes, we see the unity of our triune God and his love for his people. In Jesus's baptism, we see the Father, Son, and Spirit's inseparability in their mission to make all things new; in the Great Commission, we see the triune God's call to join that mission: to make disciples of all nations and baptize them in his name.

The doctrine of the Trinity is a call to worship, not a call to decoding mere theological facts. The name and mission of God transforms everything about us. The Father sent his Son into the world for our salvation. The Son secured our salvation and brought us into God's family and mission. The Spirit is sent to live within us, empowering us to join this mission. We are not called to save anyone from their sins; this is the work of the triune God, the power of *his* name and not ours. And yet, as he has throughout all human history, God uses broken people in his mission to unbreak all things and make the world whole again. By our triune God's authority and equipping, we carry his name and mission to the ends of the earth.

A PRAYER

Father, who dwells in an unapproachable light, you made us to be your image-bearers on earth. Grant that we would obey your Son and Spirit, spreading the good news of the gospel to the ends of the earth. In Jesus's name, by the Spirit we pray. Amen.

CHAPTER FOUR

The Word Made Flesh
JOHN 1:1-18

In our culture, every sector of life feels like a rivalry. Our companies, favorite sports teams, clothing brands, and, sadly, even our churches often seem to be in competition with others. We feel a sense of rivalry at times with coworkers or neighbors who outshine us in some capacity. At the heart of it all is some combination of sinful pride and greed.

It is hard for us as mere mortals to comprehend a God who is truly unrivaled and who claims to be unrivaled with no sense of pride. Even theologically, we can mistakenly assume Satan is some sort of peer to God when we speak about the struggle between light and darkness, good and evil. Biblically, we see that Israel's neighbors thought their gods were rivals to our God. But our God is unmatched. For example, we see his power on full display in his rescue of the Israelites from Egypt's vast army (Exod 14) and in his defeat of Baal and his many prophets (1 Kgs 18:20–40). He alone stands above and beyond creation. He alone is self-sufficient and all-powerful. He alone is in a category with no rivals. He alone is worthy of our worship.

His incomparable power and authority are fundamentally rooted in the first words of the Bible: "In the beginning God created the heavens and the earth" (Gen 1:1). Before all things, there was the triune God. And then God created all things—heaven, earth, and every single thing that dwells in and around them—by his Word and with the presence of his Spirit (Gen 1:2–3). Simply put: creation is everything that is not God.

This confession sets God apart from all of creation. And the creator/creature distinction means that God is uniquely worthy of honor and submission.[14] In Psalm 115, for example, the psalmist declares,

> Not to us, LORD, not to us,
>> but to your name give glory
>> because of your faithful love, because of your
>>> truth.

Why should the nations say,
    "Where is their God?"
Our God is in heaven
    and does whatever he pleases.
Their idols are silver and gold,
    made by human hands.
They have mouths but cannot speak,
    eyes, but cannot see.
They have ears but cannot hear,
    noses, but cannot smell.
They have hands but cannot feel,
    feet, but cannot walk.
    They cannot make a sound with their throats.
Those who make them are just like them,
    as are all who trust in them. (Ps 115:1–8)

God is unrestrained by creation and thus worthy of our worship and adoration. No one can stand against God. God laughs a holy laugh at any insinuation that he has a rival (Ps 2:4; 37:13). When we read John 1, we may become uneasy when Jesus is equated with God in the strongest of terms, but this is the mystery of the Trinity.

THE WORD, GOD WITH GOD

John 1 was crucial to the early church's understanding of the Trinity. When the doctrine of the Trinity was being articulated and defended against myriad heresies, references to John 1 were inescapable. And for good reason. This passage is rich with language about the identity of the Son and his relationship to the Father, laying out a relatively clear portrait of the two persons as distinct from one another and yet equally divine. The passage begins by talking about "the Word":

> In the beginning was the Word, and the Word was with God, and the Word was God. He was with God in the beginning. All things were created through him, and apart from him not one thing was created that has been created. (John 1:1–3)

We know this Word to be Jesus based on the rest of the passage, but it is a striking way for John to start. This "in the beginning was the Word" language reminds us of Genesis 1, in which God created all things by speaking. However, the Word in John 1 is not merely God's voice or a set of syllables; rather, the Word is a person who was "with God" and also "was God." We could think about the beginning of John's Gospel as a commentary on Genesis 1 in light of Jesus's incarnation. We will see this reiterated as the chapter progresses, but it is most obvious here.

If we try to put this plainly, we could say that this Word is distinct from God the Father ("with God") and is God the Son ("was God"), who created all things with the Father. For the Jewish monotheist, this sets up a difficult dilemma: if God is *one* and the creator, how can there be another person who is also God? Are there now two Gods? Is the Old Testament simply not true anymore now that Jesus has come?

The early church was doggedly committed to preserving the idea that God is one. As we have seen, the Scriptures are abundantly clear about this. To deny the oneness of God and his unique role as creator would be to deny the plain truth of Scripture. However, to deny that Jesus is also God who created all things would be to deny the plain truth of John 1, which is also Scripture. Since they believed that the Bible is true and authoritative, they worked to make sense of this mystery. Their decision, ultimately, was to say that we must affirm that God is one and that the Father and Son are both eternally divine persons. Scripture's claims pressure us to say both, thus both must be true.

To say, for example, that "the Word" is a creation of the Father would imply that God was once mute or unable to speak. But since God is all-powerful, wholly perfect, and unchanging (Ps 33:11; Mal 3:6), we can only assume that this Word is also eternal. We cannot add powers or abilities or attributes to a God who is already whole. To add to God is to say that God has a weakness.

The key, then, is to have humility to know that God is incomprehensible. As Gregory of Nazianzus put it: one day we will know God more fully (1 Cor 13:12), "but for the present what reaches us is … a small beam from a great light."[15] Gregory was adamant that this "small beam" was God's revelation to us about himself, so we cannot merely say that we cannot know *anything*. But his point is that we cannot put God in a petri dish or run him through a mathematical algorithm; to think we can fully analyze him like any other subject is to make God part of creation rather than the creator. We can only speak as far as his revelation in Scripture will allow. So, we are not required to be silent about who God is, but we are required to not speak beyond what has been revealed through the words and patterns of Scripture.

After saying that Jesus was with God, was/is God, and created all things just like God, John's language continues to hammer home Jesus's divinity: "In him was life, and that life was the light of men. That light shines in the darkness, and yet the darkness did not overcome it" (John 1:4–5). John claims here that life is found in Jesus. This reiterates the language about Jesus as creator and echoes the biblical witness about God as the self-sufficient giver of life and on whom all life depends (see Gen 2:7; Neh 9:6; Job 10:12; Ps 36:9). Jesus is the divine life-giver who created all things and on whom all creation depends. This is repeated in John 1:10–13, as well, speaking of those who rejected his offer of life as their creator.

Moreover, he is the light that shines in the darkness, as Scripture claims about God in places like Micah 7:8: "Do not rejoice over me, my enemy! Though I have fallen, I will stand up; though I sit in darkness, the LORD will be my light." Though the world is darkened by sin and death, God brings light into the darkness, a light so bright that the sun will be essentially useless one day (Rev 22:5). Again, drawing on Genesis 1, life is given, and the distinction between light and darkness is made clear. In just a few sentences, John has already described Jesus with fundamental divine attributes: he is eternal, the creator, the life-giver, and the light in darkness.

Next, Jesus is called "the Word" once again, but now John highlights his incarnation:

The Word became flesh and dwelt among us. We observed his glory, the glory as the one and only Son from the Father, full of grace and truth. (John testified concerning him and exclaimed, "This was the one of whom I said, 'The one coming after me ranks ahead of me, because he existed before me.'") Indeed, we have all received grace upon grace from his fullness, for the law was given through Moses; grace and truth came through Jesus Christ. No one has ever seen God. The one and only Son, who is himself God and is at the Father's side—he has revealed him. (John 1:14–18)

The Word that is the eternal creator, beyond spatial boundaries, has now stepped into his own creation to bring divine light into our sinful darkness. Of course, God has always descended to his people, most obviously in the garden of Eden, pillar of fire/cloud, tabernacle, temple, and always with his Word. And when God the Son came in the flesh, "We observed his glory, the glory as the one and only Son from the Father, full of grace and truth" (John 1:14).

Throughout the Old Testament, it is God whose glory is too intense for Moses to behold (Exod 33:18–23) and whose glory is not shared with anyone (Isa 42:8). For mankind to be able to behold the glory of God in the face of Jesus, we are left with confessing that Jesus must be God in the flesh, and that somehow the Father and Son are both fully God and yet distinct persons. Moses (or anyone else) could not look directly at God on the mountain as a mere human, but "the one and only Son, who is himself God and is at the Father's side—he has revealed him" (John 1:18). As God's Son, the Father's glory is his glory; as God-made-flesh, he can reveal that glory to mankind in a way once considered unthinkable. As Richard Bauckham said of Jesus's place on the creator side of the creator/creature divide, "What Christ does, God does."[16]

As I mentioned above, this passage was foundational for the early church as they sought to articulate the biblical Trinity. One needs to look no further than one of the oldest confessions in church history, the Nicene Creed. Below is a portion of the Creed, which reads like a theological summary of John 1 (though many other passages were no doubt influential):

> And in one Lord Jesus Christ,
>> the only Son of God,
>> begotten from the Father before all ages,
> God from God,
> Light from Light,
>> true God from true God,
>> begotten, not made;
>> of the same essence as the Father.
> Through him all things were made.
> For us and for our salvation
>> he came down from heaven;
>> he became incarnate by the Holy Spirit and the
>>> virgin Mary,
>> and was made human.

This confession was more than a way to pass some theological exam. It was a call to worship. As Athanasius of

Alexandria, a key figure in these early debates about Jesus's divinity, noted: to deny the divinity of Jesus is to show "a lack of reverence and ignorance of God."[17] If Jesus is this divine person—eternal creator, true God from true God— then worship is the only appropriate response.

When Jesus asked Peter, "Who do you say that I am?" (Matt 16:15), he sought an answer. He was not a mere prophet or wise sage as some thought—he was much more. Peter said, rightly, that he is "the Messiah, the Son of the living God." Because he truly is God, he is worthy of our worship and has the power to save us from our sins; because he is truly human, he is able to truly be the obedient second Adam who bled, died, raised, and ascended in our place.

A PRAYER

Father, you give every good thing. Because you sent your only begotten Son, we can be your sons and daughters. Grant that we would listen to your Son and praise him. In Jesus's name, by the Spirit we pray. Amen.

CHAPTER FIVE

The Father and Son Give Life

JOHN 5:17-30

At the beginning of every semester, a colleague of mine takes his freshman students to a cemetery next to campus. As they stand amid headstones marked with the span of each deceased person's life, he challenges them to consider their mortality. Young people think they are going to live forever, he says; but the truth is we are "like a vapor that appears for a little while, then vanishes" (Jas 4:14). While this may sound a little odd to some, it is a jarring way to help young people take stock of their plans and priorities.

From the earliest pages of the Bible, God shows himself to be a God of life. As we saw in our discussion of John 1, this life-giving power and prerogative belongs solely to the Lord. The Levites in Nehemiah 9 offer us the clearest picture of Israel's experience with God's life-giving work, noting the many ways he provided for their ancestors. They begin with a confessional summary:

> Blessed be the LORD your God from everlasting to
> everlasting.
> Blessed be your glorious name,
>> and may it be exalted above all blessing and
>> praise.
> You, LORD, are the only God.
> You created the heavens,
>> the highest heavens with all their stars,
>> the earth and all that is on it,
>> the seas and all that is in them.
> You give life to all of them,
>> and all the stars of heaven worship you. (Neh
>> 9:5–6)

As the creator, God *just is* the life-giver. Death has no claim on his people.

Jesus's claim to be a life-giver is another example of how his words and deeds confounded those (seemingly) most able to understand them. The problem starts when he heals a man on the Sabbath, which was supposed to be a day of rest (John 5:1–16). When asked by the Jewish leaders why he was working on the rest day, he replied simply, "My Father is still working, and I am working also" (John 5:17). Jesus's words here seem tamer than his claim in Matthew 12:8 ("the Son of man is Lord of the Sabbath"), but the point rings the same in their ears: Jesus was "making himself equal to God" (John 5:18). Blasphemy once again.

This passage gets a bit tricky as Jesus explains what he means, but there is much to glean about the Trinity as it relates to the Father and Son's relationship. Before we get too far, it is worth noting again that Jesus is God incarnate—the Word who became flesh. Since Jesus is fully God, he cannot become less than God, because God cannot change. So, when we say he "put on flesh," we are acknowledging that, in the mystery of the incarnation, Jesus is both truly God and truly man. As we discussed in our chapter on Philippians 2, for example, is a helpful summary the Chalcedonian Definition's language of "two natures, without confusion, without change, without division, without separation." Jesus did not put his divinity aside or pretend to be human; he was no less "equal to God" even as he truly walked, talked, slept, and ate in first-century Greco-Roman towns.

This Chalcedonian principle is important to remember in this passage because it helps us make sense of how the Bible speaks of Jesus's divine and human natures. After all, what confounds the Jewish leaders is how *a man* can claim to be equal to God; this amazes some (Matt 9:8), but causes others to rage against him (John 5:18). This principle will also help us make sense of his response to the charge of blasphemy.[18]

Once again, Jesus does not back down from their charge. There is no apology, no clarification. They are absolutely right to say that Jesus is making himself equal to God. The Father and Son share such equality that:

> the Son is not able to do anything on his own, but only what he sees the Father doing. For whatever the Father does, the Son likewise does these things. For the Father loves the Son and shows him everything he is doing, and he will show him greater works than these so that you will be amazed. (John 5:19–20)

Some might think that Jesus is merely a special man, and therefore he has a special status to do what the Father asks. But this is not a statement about some kind of divine hierarchy, as though Jesus is a mere man or even a lesser god who siphons power from the Father. That type of statement would confirm their assumption that he *is not* equal to the Father, an assumption he readily challenges here and elsewhere. Rather, it is a statement about the Son's ability to do whatever the Father does—a statement about shared power and activity.

Jesus continues to affirm his equality with God, saying, "And just as the Father raises the dead and gives them life, so the Son also gives life to whom he wants" (John 5:21). If there was any doubt that Jesus is clearly claiming equality with God, that doubt should be smashed to pieces here. Whatever it might mean for Jesus to say, "I do what the Father is doing," or "the Father shows me amazing things," it doesn't mean that he is simply subordinate or inferior to the Father. We know this because Jesus claims divine prerogatives for himself, saying that he "gives life *to whom he wants*." In sum, then, we can say that the Father and Son work inseparably as "one" (they are both "working"), and yet are both divine persons ("three," along with the Spirit) who exercise divine power and prerogatives (they both give life to whomever they want). Jesus shows this life-giving power and prerogative in other places, such as the raising of his friend Lazarus (John 11:38–44), and it is clear that Jesus doesn't need to call on the Father in order to borrow some resurrection power.

How can Jesus give life to the dead, a claim proper only to God? "For just as the Father has life in himself, so also he has granted to the Son to have life in himself" (John 5:26). Again, we see unity between the Father and Son, a shared power of self-sufficiency. The Father has life in himself; the Son has life in himself. Jesus is equal to God because only God can create and sustain life. Harkening back to Genesis 1 and John 1, Jesus says that he can speak life into existence; moreover, he will one day exercise that power fully when he returns to defeat sin and death, resurrect the dead, enact divine judgment in unity with the Father, and bring his people back to the tree of life (John 5:24–30; Rev 19–22).

LIFE IN THE SON

The Son came to us in order to give us life. His sinless life, death, burial, resurrection, ascension, and intercession secure our eternal life. And this gift of life is a Trinitarian work, as seen in the resurrection of Jesus himself. Scripture says that the Father raised Jesus from the dead (Gal 1:1), the Holy Spirit raised Jesus from the dead (Rom 8:11; 1 Pet 3:19), and Jesus said that he has the power to raise himself (John 10:18). *The triune God* raised Jesus from the dead.

Jesus says in our passage that "anyone who hears my word and believes him who sent me has eternal life and will not come under judgment but has passed from death to life" (John 5:24). As God, he can make that claim because he has the divine power and authority over life and death; as man, he died a true death and rose again to secure our resurrection (1 Cor 15). Death could not hold the author of life; therefore death cannot hold those who hear his voice and believe in his name.

A PRAYER

Father, you are the God of life. Your Son defeated death with his death so that we might have life. Give us this life. In Jesus's name, by the Spirit we pray. Amen.

CHAPTER SIX

I AM
JOHN 8:58

I worked with a pastor who often (mostly jokingly) reminded me that he was older and wiser than me. When we would have friendly debates about theology or church-related issues, a stalemate would end with: "Well, Brandon, I was thinking about this issue when you were still in diapers." It was an excellent way to break any tension, but it also was a good lesson for me to be humble and restrained in my youthful zeal.

We all live within the constraints of time and space. In this life, we do our best to gain knowledge, develop wisdom, and learn from our mistakes. But God doesn't work like this. Because he is the eternal creator who created time and space itself, he is not bound like we are. His knowledge and wisdom are perfect. And this is good news for us, if we are willing to humble ourselves.

When God commissions Moses to free his people from slavery in Egypt, Moses humbly replies, "Who am I that I should go to Pharaoh and that I should bring the Israelites out of Egypt?" (Exod 3:11). God's answer to this question would set the trajectory for Israel's post-Egyptian future and carry all the way to the church today: "I will certainly be with you" (Exod 3:12). Moses is a mere man—he cannot lead his people out of Egypt on his own, but this one speaking from the bush can:

> God replied to Moses, "I AM WHO I AM. This is what you are to say to the Israelites: I AM has sent me to you." God also said to Moses, "Say this to the Israelites: The LORD, the God of your ancestors, the God of Abraham, the God of Isaac, and the God of Jacob, has sent me to you. This is my name forever; this is how I am to be remembered in every generation. (Exod 3:14–15)

I AM WHO I AM

God explains what this name means: he is the God of their ancestors, and his name is eternal. He was there before them; he will be there after them. He is past, present, and future; he is eternal, beyond time and space, beyond any limitation. This creator God who stands outside of all creaturely boundaries has nonetheless drawn near to his people. If they have any doubt that he can succeed, they only need to trust that *he is* and there is no chance the Egyptians, with all their power and might, could ever hold him back. His power exceeds the greatest opposition humanity could ever mount against him. There is one God—I AM—who alone is worthy of worship, the only one worthy of reverence for his power, might, and direct acts of salvation.

In John 8:58, Jesus strikingly claims, "Before Abraham was, I am." As we have seen many times before, Jesus claims divine titles and attributes intentionally and without apology. And as we have also seen, Jesus's claims have a particular inflection that frustrates and confuses those well-versed in the Old Testament.

I AM BEFORE ABRAHAM

The Jewish leaders are confronted once again with Jesus claiming to be equal with God. One of the common tactics they employ (seen here and in other passages we've discussed) is trying to trap Jesus in a contradiction or outright lie. Jesus is accused of doing his work by the power of Satan.

Jesus predictably and noticeably does not back down. Once again, he reiterates his equality with the Father:

"I do not have a demon," Jesus answered. "On the contrary, I honor my Father and you dishonor me. I do not seek my own glory; there is one who seeks it and judges. Truly I tell you, if anyone keeps my word, he will never see death." (John 8:49–51)

The relationship between the Father and Son is a common refrain in John's Gospel. He does not merely equate their work but the divine power and authority behind the work. He has been sent by the Father and therefore has the power and authority of the Father in himself (John 5:26). The implication is that dishonoring Jesus is equal to dishonoring the Father, for both are worthy of divine honor.

Jesus honors the Father by revealing the Father perfectly in the flesh (as only the God-man can do) and has the divine power over life and death (John 5:24–27). Because of this reality, to believe in Jesus is to believe in the Father; or, put more directly, to believe in Jesus is to believe in *God*. Jesus never allows anyone to separate himself and the Father, because he and the Father are one and have always been one. He is the eternal Son, the one who inseparably and equally created all things and in whom all things hold together (John 1:1–3; Col 1:17).

The Jews are understandably confused. Those who believed in God, like the great Abraham, ultimately died; how can Jesus say that he will never die or that anyone who follows him will never die (John 8:52–53)? They may be thinking, "He is putting himself above God!" But Jesus is simply thinking bigger than them, trying to show them that salvation is even more than they might imagine.

Jesus says elsewhere, "I am the way, the truth, and the life. No one comes to the Father except through me" (John 14:6). God's work of salvation is inextricably tied to the Father and Son's inseparable nature and work. Jesus once again explains his unique relationship to the Father to bring the point home:

> "If I glorify myself," Jesus answered, "my glory is nothing. My Father—about whom you say, 'He is our God'—he is the one who glorifies me. You do not know him, but I know him. If I were to say I don't know him, I would be a liar like you. But I do know him, and I keep his word. Your father Abraham rejoiced to see my day; he saw it and was glad." (John 8:54–56)

It might be tempting to read this passage and think that Jesus is saying that he is there to pass along God's glory, as though he is only a messenger. However, we can note two things at this point that lend themselves toward a clear Trinitarian account.

First, we saw in John 1:14 that divine glory belongs to Jesus just as it belongs to the Father: "We have observed *his* glory, the glory as the one and only Son from the Father." Second, we see here that the Father glorifies Jesus, not that Jesus exclusively points to the Father in a one-way fashion; we see that the Father also points to the Son and his glory. So, Jesus tells them plainly that if they worship God, then they should accept that Jesus is equal to him. Why? Because the Father has sent him and has in turn shown the world the Son's divine nature and attributes. There is a reciprocal glorification between the Father and Son that clearly shows their inseparable power, authority, and ability to save.

Jesus also tells them that Abraham looked forward to his incarnation, as though Abraham himself glorified Jesus as he looked forward to the day God's Messiah would come. Their two great "fathers"—Yahweh himself and their ancestral father Abraham—both point to Jesus for the way to salvation and eternal life. If Jesus were only a man, and particularly a mere man who is working for the devil, how is it that God himself puts Jesus on par with God? Jesus is tearing apart their logic one step at a time. And, amazingly, Jesus has not said the most shocking thing yet.

The Jews clearly understand that Jesus is claiming equality with the Father, so they pull out one last trump card: "The Jews replied, 'You aren't fifty years old yet, and you've seen Abraham?'" (John 8:57–58).

Jesus said to them, "Truly I tell you, before Abraham was, I am" (John 8:58). As we have seen, "I AM" carries a very particular connotation for the Jews. If there was any doubt that Jesus was claiming the name of Yahweh himself, we only need to look at how the Jews respond to this statement: "So they picked up stones to throw at him. But Jesus was hidden and went out of the temple" (John 8:59). While we are not sure exactly what it meant for Jesus to suddenly be "hidden" from them, the point is that he was escaping yet another attempt at being assaulted for blasphemy. The people most ripe for seeing their own God in the flesh were the first to turn from him.

GLORIFYING THE SON

God's people read Israel's Scriptures but had difficulty understanding Jesus's claims about his fulfillment of those Scriptures. As Christians on the other side of the New Testament, now reading the two-Testament witness to our triune God, we have the benefit of hindsight. While it may be easy to shake our heads at the Jews for not seeing their Messiah—their God—standing in front of them, our doubt and indignation can creep up when Jesus challenges us.

Like the Jews, we may be tempted to blaspheme the Son and the Holy Spirit (Mark 3:28–30), not being willing to accept their words and deeds. But if we claim to worship God, then we will glorify the Father, Son, and Holy Spirit precisely because they glorify one another. It is our triune God who tells us how to worship rightly—which means giving equal glory and honor to the Father, Son, and Holy Spirit.

A PRAYER

Father, we have seen your glory in the words and works of your Son. By his words and works bring us from death into life. In Jesus's name, by the Spirit we pray. Amen.

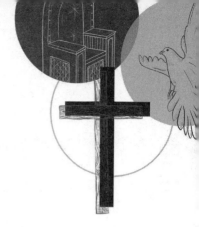

CHAPTER SEVEN

The Comforter
JOHN 14-16

Most of us have experienced the sadness of moving away from family and friends (or vice versa). While the relationship doesn't end simply because of relocation, we know the benefits of embodied presence over against letters, text messages, or even video chats. Nothing replaces being face to face with those we love most.

Imagine the disciples' surprise when Jesus told them he would be leaving them soon. Not only that, but that it would be *better* for him to go. Like us, they knew that him leaving would be devastating. He was not only their friend, but their Lord. And in the first century, they could not lean on today's technology to see each other face-to-face even from a distance. When Jesus ascended, he didn't go away to another town or country; he ascended upward and out of their sight (Acts 1). The promised Holy Spirit would come soon, however, and the promise in Joel 2:28–29 would be fulfilled (Acts 2).

In the first words of the Bible, the Holy Spirit makes his first appearance:

> In the beginning God created the heavens and the earth. Now the earth was formless and empty, darkness covered the surface of the watery depths, and the Spirit of God was hovering over the surface of the waters. (Gen 1:1–2)

This "Spirit of God," active in the moment of creation, indicates that his presence among his people was immediate and real. It's a stark affirmation that God is not some distant creator but intimately engaged in his creation. By Genesis 3, Adam and Eve have sinned and been expelled from the garden, and yet God is with them even then. As the Old Testament progresses, we see numerous examples of God's presence among his people—in the wilderness, in the tabernacle, and through the prophets.

Isaiah says God's people often "rebelled and grieved his Holy Spirit." Nonetheless he "put his Holy Spirit among the flock" and "the Spirit of the LORD gave them rest" (Isa 63:10–14). In fact, God reminds his people through

Haggai: "This is the promise I made to you when you came out of Egypt, and my Spirit is present among you; don't be afraid" (Hag 2:5).

God never leaves his people. If the Holy Spirit has been God's tangible presence among his people throughout their history, surely the Spirit's descending on Jesus at his baptism and the pouring out of the Spirit at Pentecost are continuations of the same story. We see this promise coming to fruition in John 14–16.

SENDING THE COMFORTER

To understand the Trinity—and particularly the person of the Holy Spirit—we cannot separate the persons into distinct actors at different times in history. The Father, Son, and Holy Spirit work inseparably, so there has never been a time in which one of the Trinitarian persons was taking a day off, as it were, or waiting to be called off the bench to get into the action. Indeed God—the triune God—"does not slumber or sleep" (Ps 121:4). The unity and distinction of the Trinity is a mystery we cannot fully comprehend, but the revelation of God in the Scriptures pressures us to keep a healthy balance between affirming that God is both one and yet three.

Gregory of Nyssa helps with framing as we consider John 14–16 and the person of the Holy Spirit. In one place, he says:

The Son is the Father's power (1 Cor 1.24). Those therefore who are saved through the Son are saved by the Father's Power. … Whether you look at the whole world, or at the parts of the world which constitute the whole, all these are the Father's works, produced by his Power, and thus the scripture is true in both ways, when it says both that the Father makes all things, and that without the Son no existing thing comes to be; for the activity of the Power points back to him whose Power he is. Since therefore the Son is the Father's power, all the works of the Son are the works of the Power.[19]

As we have seen throughout this book, the inseparability of the Father and Son is evident, in part, by the shared power and authority between them. Gregory then helps us understand the Holy Spirit's divinity in a similar way, noting that the power of the Father and Son is incomplete without the power of the Holy Spirit to complete their work.[20] The easiest way to understand the Holy Spirit's divinity and personhood is to see how he is intimately involved in the triune God's work in ways no human, angel, or any other creature is.

In John 14–16, Jesus gives multiple examples and discourses that reveal the Holy Spirit's work in salvation, particularly the ways in which Jesus will work inseparably from the Holy Spirit even after his ascension. After his classic line—"I am the way, the truth, and the life. No one comes to the Father except through me" (John 14:6)—Jesus reiterates the inseparability of his work and the Father's when Philip asks to see the Father:

> Jesus said to him, "Have I been among you all this time and you do not know me, Philip? The one who has seen me has seen the Father. How can you say, 'Show us the Father'? Don't you believe that I am in the Father and the Father is in me? The words I speak to you I do not speak on my own. The Father who lives in me does his works. Believe me that I am in the Father and the Father is in me. Otherwise, believe because of the works themselves." (John 14:9–11)

Notice that Jesus points to his works as proof that he is who he says he is. If you have any doubt about his divinity and equality with the Father, watch how he speaks and acts with the same power and authority. This is crucial as he moves to the next point.

Jesus then tells them that he would be leaving, but not entirely:

> I will not leave you as orphans; I am coming to you. In a little while the world will no longer see me, but you will see me. Because I live, you will live too. On

that day you will know that I am in my Father, you are in me, and I am in you. The one who has my commands and keeps them is the one who loves me. And the one who loves me will be loved by my Father. I also will love him and will reveal myself to him. (John 14:18–21)

How could this be? How could Jesus leave them and yet ... come to them? Because "the Counselor, the Holy Spirit, whom the Father will send in my name, will teach you all things and remind you of everything I have told you" (John 14:26). When the Holy Spirit is among them, so is Jesus (and the Father). And the Holy Spirit will be another Counselor or "Comforter" (KJV) who will remind them of all things.

In John 15, Jesus continues preparing them for his departure. First, he tells them that they are to abide in him, leaning on him for their comfort in the midst of the coming persecution for being his disciples. This will not be easy, but "when the Counselor comes, the one I will send to you from the Father—the Spirit of truth who proceeds from the Father—he will testify about me" (John 15:26). Just as Jesus is the only begotten Son of God— the eternal Son who has no beginning—so too the Holy Spirit eternally proceeds from the Father. He has been with God since the beginning and will continue his work of bringing comfort to God's people, as he did throughout Israel's history.

Then, in John 16:7, Jesus says perhaps the most surprising statement: "It is for your benefit that I go away, because if I don't go away the Counselor will not come to you. If I go, I will send him to you." It is one thing to encourage them that the Holy Spirit will be the Father and Son's presence among them—this might be a bandage on the wound until he returns. But he says it is *for their benefit*—it is better—for him to go away. Why? If he does not go away, the Holy Spirit will not come to complete his work. We don't know his works, but God does, and Jesus says it plainly.

To recap, then, the Trinitarian dynamic goes like this: the Father sends the Son, and they work inseparably and with equal power and authority. If you have seen the Son, you have seen the Father; the Father glorifies the Son, and the Son glorifies the Father. And then, the Holy Spirit, who has been among God's people since the very beginning, will be sent by the Father and Son (cf. John 15:26) to continue and complete the work of the Father and Son. Where the Holy Spirit is, there also are the Father and Son. The disciples need not worry because Jesus's ascension is not the end of their story nor the end of God's bigger story; rather, the Holy Spirit will come and empower them to do what Jesus did—proclaim the gospel, heal the sick, cast out demons, and advance the triune God's story of redeeming creation. The Spirit of God is the presence of God among the people of God in their wandering, suffering, and even rebellion.

THE PRESENCE OF THE COMFORTER

The story of God's people is in many ways the story of a wandering, suffering, and rebellious people. There are no perfect people—this is why the Son put on flesh and dwelt among us, to be the perfect human in our place. The cross shows us that there are no shortcuts to salvation.

The comfort, however, is the truth that our triune God never leaves us. Though we are intent to destroy ourselves and everything around us, he is faithful to keep moving history toward redemption. When he makes a covenant, he keeps it. When we break the covenant, he still keeps it. Though he may feel distant at times, we know he has never left us—Pentecost is proof. Every promise of God has come true, and the Holy Spirit brings the triune God's comforting presence into our hearts, come what may.

A PRAYER

Father, we are sinners. Your Son forgives our sins and gives us life. By your Spirit, teach us to pray and believe. In Jesus's name, by the Spirit we pray. Amen.

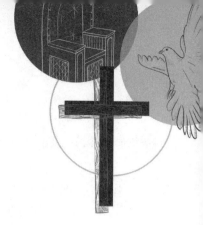

CHAPTER EIGHT

Resurrection and Adoption
ROMANS 8

If you have adopted a child or known someone who has, you know the joy of seeing a child be welcomed into a loving family. Many tears are shed when the judge announces to the room that the child is officially adopted—officially brought out of chaos and instability and welcomed into what should be a loving, stable, healthy home. In some ways, it is a promise of new life. Christians and non-Christians alike recognize the importance and beauty of a loving home for children. For Christians, however, we have the hope of being adopted into God's family.

The familial language God uses for his children—from Israel, to his only begotten Son, to each of us—is one of deep love and care. Not only does he build his family through the election of a nation, but he uses that nation to draw in people from other nations. God's adoption is one of gathering people from everywhere, even those who appear to have no place in his family. He tells the Israelites to welcome the sojourner and exile, to be the vehicle through which God blesses the world and expands the family of God. For example, he tells Israel to treat non-Israelites as "native-born." Why? Because Israel was itself once a nation without a home (Lev 19:33–34). When God adopts someone into his family, they are treated as though they are native-born, flesh-and-blood brothers and sisters.

Though the Son is distinct from us as a divine person and as the only begotten Son of God, we are nonetheless adopted into God's family—Jew and gentile alike—and promised a new life and a new home (John 14:2; Rev 21–22). We see a picture of this adoption and new life in Romans 8, in which Paul uses familial language to discuss the expanding portrait of the triune God's family.

TRIUNE RESURRECTION AND ADOPTION

Understanding the Bible's two-Testament witness to the triune God is primarily an exercise in bringing together various themes and patterns to show how the one God is

Father, Son, and Holy Spirit. Sometimes, however, passages will bring together all three persons with relative clarity and depth. We saw this, for example, in Matthew 3:13–17 and John 14–16. Romans 8 is another example of a passage that clearly shows the triune God's inseparable work.

Paul shifts from the effects of sin in Romans 7 to the good news of the gospel here in chapter 8. In the first few verses, we immediately see a Trinitarian picture:

> Therefore, there is now no condemnation for those in Christ Jesus, because the law of the Spirit of life in Christ Jesus has set you free from the law of sin and death. For what the law could not do since it was weakened by the flesh, God did. He condemned sin in the flesh by sending his own Son in the likeness of sinful flesh as a sin offering, in order that the law's requirement would be fulfilled in us who do not walk according to the flesh but according to the Spirit. (Rom 8:1–4)

Salvation is a Trinitarian act. The law cannot save us, and we cannot save ourselves, but our triune God can save us. The Father sent the Son to be the obedient second Adam because of our disobedience (Rom 5:12–21), and those who believe him have been united with the Son by the Holy Spirit. Through the Son sent by the Father, we walk in the power and freedom of the Holy Spirit. Paul will reiterate this point several times throughout the passage.

When Paul talks about the Holy Spirit, he uses several different titles. For example, he uses two different titles within a few words of each other that indicate the inseparable work of the Holy Spirit with the Father and Son:

> You, however, are not in the flesh, but in the Spirit, if indeed the Spirit of God lives in you. If anyone does not have the Spirit of Christ, he does not belong to him. Now if Christ is in you, the body is dead because of sin, but the Spirit gives life because of righteousness. (Rom 8:9–10)

He is both the "Spirit of God"—the Father, in this context—and the "Spirit of Christ." These titles further clarify the Holy Spirit's distinct relationship to the Father and Son. As Basil of Caesarea asked, "Who is not lifted up in his soul and who does not raise his thoughts to the highest nature when he hears the names of the Spirit?"[21] The Holy Spirit's name(s) and work indicate that he is a distinct person from the Father and Son and yet inseparable from their nature and work. Only God can complete the work of God; only God can do what God does.

Paul moves on to talk about the triune God's work in resurrection. While many of us rightly and primarily celebrate the resurrection of Jesus on Easter—the Son put on flesh, not the Father or Holy Spirit—Paul indicates that this too is a Trinitarian act: "And if the Spirit of him who raised Jesus from the dead lives in you, then he who raised Christ from the dead will also bring your mortal bodies to life through his Spirit who lives in you" (Rom 8:11).

As we discussed in John 5, the Father and Son have the power and authority over life itself. Paul tells us here that the Holy Spirit also has this power and authority. The "Spirit of [the Father] who raised Christ from the dead" also brings life to us now and in our future resurrection. Paul talks about salvation, resurrection, and the new life in Christ all within the context of the inseparable work of the Trinitarian persons. The Holy Spirit is the glue between Jesus's resurrection and our resurrection. Without the Holy Spirit, there is no resurrection; no new life; no hope. It is by the power and authority of the Spirit of God and Christ—a power and authority inseparable from God and Christ—that "you put to death the deeds of the body, [so that] you will live" (Rom 8:13).

This new life is intricately connected to our adoption as God's sons and daughters. Being brought into God's family is the reality of this new life—the loving, stable, healthy home we were meant to have. Regardless of our own family background—healthy at times, unhealthy in others—we are adopted into God's family and promised a new life that our earthly family cannot offer, even if they wanted to. Our new life in the Holy Spirit is tied to our adoption into the family of our triune God:

> For all those led by God's Spirit are God's sons. For you did not receive a spirit of slavery to fall back into fear. Instead, you received the Spirit of adoption, by whom we cry out, "Abba, Father!" The Spirit himself testifies together with our spirit that we are God's children, and if children, also heirs—heirs of God and coheirs with Christ—if indeed we suffer with him so that we may also be glorified with him. (Rom 8:14–17)

We are adopted into the Father's family by his Son—coheirs of their kingdom—because of the Holy Spirit's work. The Holy Spirit's work is so important, so powerful, that Paul says, "The Spirit also helps us in our weakness, because we do not know what to pray for as we should, but the Spirit himself intercedes for us with inexpressible groanings" (Rom 8:26). Even when we do not know what to pray or we are too overwhelmed with longing for future resurrection, the Holy Spirit speaks on our behalf.

As we pass through this world as "sojourners and exiles" (1 Pet 2:11 ESV), we have a God who does the work—from creation to new creation—to ensure our place in God's family. And in the more immediate context of Paul's letter to the Romans, he repeatedly draws on the Old Testament theme that God has always intended his family to include Jews and gentiles—that adoption as sons and daughters is a level playing field. Again, as he reminded the Israelites in Leviticus 19:33–34, even Israel was once not a native-born son. Through the Father's love, expressed in sending the Son, and sealed by the Holy Spirit (Eph 1:3–14), we are promised adoption and resurrection in the power and authority of the triune God.

WALKING BY THE SPIRIT OF GOD AND CHRIST

From Israel to the church, God's people have been called into one family. God created Adam and Eve as the heads of one humanity; he appointed Abraham as the head of many nations; he called Israel out of Egypt to be his son; and ultimately the Father sent the Son to reconcile the world to himself, so that anyone who calls on the name of the Father's Son by the power of the Holy Spirit will be adopted and given an eternal hope of new life.

As Christians, we are to heed Paul's words: to walk by the Holy Spirit that we may walk in the life promised by our triune God. We have died with Christ and have been raised with him (Rom 6:4), and it is no longer we who live but Christ who lives in us (Gal 2:20). This work is completed and applied by the sending of the Holy Spirit. We see in this passage that our triune God has done all the work necessary to bring us redemption, and he will continue to do the work necessary to bring us all the way home to the New Jerusalem.

A PRAYER

Father, by your Son and Spirit you have brought us into your family. Grant us joy and comfort in this truth. In Jesus's name, by the Spirit we pray. Amen.

CHAPTER NINE

The Mind of God
1 CORINTHIANS 2

Michel de Nostredame—known popularly as Nostradamus—was an astrologer and physician in the sixteenth century. He is best known, however, for his prolific publications of prophesies, leading some to use his name as a shorthand for wisdom or clairvoyance. Over the following centuries, some believed his prophecies came true during the French Revolution, the rise of Hitler's Germany, and the assassination of President John F. Kennedy. A recent work, however, points out that Nostradamus's prophecies are mostly filled with vague claims that are easily manipulated by interpreters, as well as regurgitations of various well-known prophecies and sayings that are not original to him.[22] In short, Nostradamus's so-called wisdom was primarily built on human wisdom—notably, wisdom from other people that Nostradamus repackaged into his own subjective claims.

When God's people are tempted to rely on their own wisdom or even the wisdom of others, they are reminded that God's wisdom is from the vantage point of the one being who sees all, knows all, and can do all. And this divine wisdom is not hidden from us. It is not an unattainable secret that God brags about but never shows; rather, this wisdom can be obtained—perhaps not perfectly, but nonetheless genuinely—by seeking the Lord.

Scripture promised that one day God would send "the root of Jesse," someone who embodied and perfectly lived out God's wisdom:

> The Spirit of the LORD will rest on him—
>> the Spirit of wisdom and of understanding,
>> the Spirit of counsel and of might,
>> the Spirit of the knowledge and fear of the LORD—
>> and he will delight in the fear of the LORD.
>> (Isa 11:2–3 NIV)

Paul says that this "root of Jesse" is none other than Jesus Christ, through whom God will "fill you with all joy and peace as you believe so that you may overflow with hope by the power of the Holy Spirit" (Rom 15:12–13). Paul explains this promised revelation of the triune God's wisdom more fully in 1 Corinthians 2.

WISDOM OF GOD

Paul's first letter to the Corinthians is primarily a pastoral letter written to a church that is divided. The Corinthian church was arguing over all sorts of things, but Paul pointed them to their unity in the gospel. One of the ways that Paul builds the foundation for unity is talking about the unified work of the triune God. We see a good picture of this in 1 Corinthians 2.

He begins the letter by asserting that he is not powerful in and of himself; rather, the power in his ministry comes from God's power:

> I decided to know nothing among you except Jesus Christ and him crucified. I came to you in weakness, in fear, and in much trembling. My speech and my preaching were not with persuasive words of wisdom but with a demonstration of the Spirit's power, so that your faith might not be based on human wisdom but on God's power. (1 Cor 2:1–5)

When Paul talks about his ministry, he talks about the work of Christ and God's power, which he equates with the Holy Spirit's power. God's power brings true wisdom over against human wisdom, and whoever wants God's wisdom must look to the Father, Son, and Holy Spirit—those who possess and exercise the very power of God. The Trinitarian structure of his argument is obvious from the start.

As his argument unfolds, Paul further delineates between divine wisdom and human wisdom. Christians who confess Christ and who have been filled with the Holy Spirit can only find divine wisdom—*true* wisdom—by God's power, not their own. This is striking for Paul to say, because one might look at Paul's ministry as a great human effort. But he wants to remind them that it is only because of what God has done through him. In fact, he notes that human wisdom is rooted in denying the power and work of God:

> None of the rulers of this age knew this wisdom, because if they had known it, they would not have crucified the Lord of glory. ... Now God has revealed these things to us by the Spirit, since the Spirit searches everything, even the depths of God. For who knows a person's thoughts except his spirit within him? In the same way, no one knows the thoughts of God except the Spirit of God. (1 Cor 2:8, 10–11)

We see the Trinitarian language here. First, Jesus is called "the Lord of glory," bringing to mind Old Testament declarations like Isaiah 6:3, "Holy, holy, holy is the LORD; ... his glory fills the whole earth." Second, it is God who is the glorious Lord. Third, the Holy Spirit is once again tied to the work of God himself. The Holy Spirit, Paul says, is able to reveal God's wisdom—certainly something no human or angel could do. In his descriptions of the Son and Holy Spirit, we see God at work.

Paul says, "The person without the Spirit does not receive what comes from God's Spirit, because it is foolishness to him; he is not able to understand it since it is evaluated spiritually" (1 Cor 2:14). As God's people have always been commanded, the true wisdom to understand ourselves and the world around us comes from God, who has the only perfect vantage point of reality. People like Nostradamus come and go, but "the word of our God remains forever" (Isa 40:8).

Not only are God's power and wisdom revealed to us by the Son and the Holy Spirit, but Paul says that we have intimate access, because "we have the mind of Christ" (1 Cor 2:16). This turn to Jesus almost feels out of place, given that the bulk of the chapter has focused on how the Holy Spirit, not Jesus, mediates the wisdom of God to us. But God is *one,* and therefore the Father, Son, and Holy Spirit never act apart from one another. We know that ultimately the triune God is the one who gives us divine wisdom, "so that you may discern what is the good, pleasing, and perfect will of God" (Rom 12:2). Paul has made these Trinitarian connections throughout the chapter in such a way that we can recognize both the unity of the divine persons and their personal distinctions from one another. The Son was crucified, not the Father or Holy Spirit, and yet it is all three who, with one power and action, reveal divine wisdom to us.

TRIUNE WISDOM

As we have seen, God's people have always been called to look to the Lord for wisdom. Human knowledge has never matched divine wisdom—even Adam and Eve relied on the Lord's wisdom and provision before they fell—but sin only plunges human wisdom further into weakness and futility. Paul, the man who wrote most of the New Testament, knows that he has no wisdom apart from what God himself has revealed to him.

Third-century theologian Origen of Alexandria helpfully explained that not only is God's wisdom an eternal attribute but the Son is the eternal expression of God's wisdom: "And how can one, who has learnt to know and think piously about God, think or believe that God the Father ever existed, even for a single moment, without begetting his Wisdom?"[23] The revelation of God's wisdom—grounded in the incarnation of the Son and the sending of the Holy Spirit—has been given to us in the Scriptures (2 Tim 3:16–17). It is only by the power of the triune God that we can claim to know the mind of God, to understand the reality by the Spirit, and to have the mind of Christ.

A PRAYER

Father, your wisdom is beyond all wisdom. Grant us wisdom through your Son and Spirit, so that we can walk in your ways. In Jesus's name, by the Spirit we pray. Amen.

CHAPTER TEN

A New Shema
1 CORINTHIANS 8:6

The Greco-Roman world in which the New Testament was written knew that the title "Lord" carried supreme authority. Caesar Augustus (also known as Octavian) was the first Roman emperor, reigning during Jesus's childhood (27 BC–AD 14). As became custom with the Roman Caesars, Augustus was called "Lord" and worshiped as a type of divine human. More than that, he could conceivably elevate his divine status to "son of God," perhaps above even the twelve Olympian gods of Greek religion and mythology. The Greeks might have known "the Lord" to be Caesar.

The Hebrews, on the other hand, were catechized to understand that God is one and that God alone can save. He is *the* Lord without rival. The Shema rang in the ears of Israelites for generations: "Listen, Israel: The Lord our God, the Lord is one" (Deut 6:4). The Lord is one. God reinforced this truth often. The Ten Commandments begin with the command, "Do not have other gods besides me" (Exod 20:3).

So when Paul (and other biblical writers) called Jesus "Lord," they likely challenged both the Jews and the Greeks. In 1 Corinthians 8:6, we have an example of this. Not only does Paul calls Jesus "Lord," but he includes him in a renewed Shema.

GOD AND LORD

In 1 Corinthians, Paul goes to great lengths to try to get his divided brothers and sisters to be unified on a number of issues. It seems that they are fighting about everything, including the issue in this passage: food. As the Christian message continues to spread throughout the Roman Empire, people from all walks of life are coming to faith—and bringing some of their customs and traditions with them. In particular, the issue revolves around people who have come to faith but are still willing to eat food sacrificed to idols.

Paul acknowledges up front that there should be no sacrificing to idols. This is apparently not an agree-to-disagree matter. He says plainly that "there is no God but one" (1 Cor 8:4), but he says of these idols:

> For even if there are so-called gods, whether in heaven or on earth—as there are many "gods" and many "lords"—yet for us there is one God, the Father. All things are from him, and we exist for him. (1 Cor 8:5–6a)

These are so-called gods who have no power and are not worthy of devotion. This is simple enough, right? The belief that God is *one* is at the core of the Jewish and Christian faith, so any sort of sacrifices to idols are immediately out of bounds. These idols, Paul will argue in many places, are just other created things made by the creator. There is no way they could be equal to him and therefore be worthy of worship.

What Paul says next is even more shocking: "And there is one Lord, Jesus Christ. All things are through him, and we exist through him" (1 Cor 8:6b). This statement clearly places Jesus in the "creator" category alongside the Father in opposition to idols. We could try to explain away this apparent equality between the Father and Jesus. For example, perhaps Paul is making a very clear distinction between the titles "God" and "Lord." There are two reasons why that's not the case.

First, these two titles are relatively interchangeable in the Old Testament with respect to Yahweh. We saw in 1 Kings 18 that "the Lord" *is* "God" for the Israelites, far above Baal, the false god. Here in 1 Corinthians 8, there is a similar distinction between false worship (idols, "so-called gods/lords") and true worship (God the Father and the Lord Jesus Christ). Paul's connection between the two terms seems intentional, as does this singular phrase that includes God the Father and the Lord Jesus Christ. Second, even if we grant that this is not definitive, Paul also uses creator-language for both the Father and Jesus. It is both of these persons, Paul asserts, through whom all things are made and exist.

Many scholars have pointed out that this is a "new Shema" that includes Jesus.[24] It is not as though Deuteronomy 6:4 is suddenly obsolete; rather the confession takes on a fuller meaning in light of the revelation of the eternal Son in the incarnation and resurrection. It now has a *Christian* inflection, such that you can hear Paul saying, "Listen, church, God our Father and the Lord Jesus Christ are one." The Corinthians needed to hear Paul's words to remember: to turn away from idols and toward the one God and Lord.

TURNING FROM IDOLS AND RIVALS

Jesus is God. Putting him into worship language drawing on Deuteronomy 6:4 couldn't be clearer. If he were not God, it would be idolatry; but since he is God, worship is entirely fitting.

As fallen people in a fallen world, we are tempted to fix our eyes on the world around us, forgetting to look to the God who made us and who calls us to fix our eyes on him (Heb 12:2). We are like Adam and Eve, looking for instant gratification that we have not been promised. We are like the Israelites, creating golden calves when we want to control God or when we think God is too distant to hear us. We are like the Israelites with Elijah at Mount Carmel, waiting to see if perhaps Baal can answer before God (1 Kgs 18). We are like those who stood before the resurrected Jesus and *still* doubted (Matt 28:17).

The good news is this: though we worship the idols in front of our eyes, God himself puts on flesh and stands in front of us. As Athanasius of Alexandria said so beautifully, "Although being unseen and invisible, through his works he appeared and made himself known to be the Word of the Father, the ruler and king of the universe."[25] There are no rivals to our triune God, and when we fix our eyes on him, there is no question.

A PRAYER

Father, you are the Lord our God. Turn our eyes from idols and grant us the faith to worship you with the Son and Spirit. In Jesus's name, by the Spirit we pray. Amen.

CHAPTER ELEVEN

The Ministry of the Spirit
2 CORINTHIANS 3

Y ou are cold-blooded." "You have a heart of stone." We use these phrases casually to describe someone who lacks empathy or seeks to hurt others. We are well aware of basic human anatomy—our heart and the blood it pumps are warm, fleshy, alive. Those who seem to lack basic human decency are illustrative of someone who seems nearly dead inside.

Whether we are stone-cold because we lack love for others, or whether we are rigid, stiff-necked law-keepers, we lack the true heart of being human—to freely live and love in light of the gospel. The Bible describes this disposition in various ways, but God promises to make us into people who truly live. By his power and his power alone, we have the chance to be freed from the bondage of sin and brought from death to life.

All Scripture is profitable (2 Tim 3:16–17). However, Jeremiah 31 illuminates the biblical story line in a distinct way because it promises a new covenant with God's people. And this covenant fulfills and brings into order everything the old covenants were anticipating:

> "Look, the days are coming"—this is the LORD's declaration—"when I will make a new covenant with the house of Israel and with the house of Judah. This one will not be like the covenant I made with their ancestors on the day I took them by the hand to lead them out of the land of Egypt—my covenant that they broke even though I am their master"— the LORD's declaration. "Instead, this is the covenant I will make with the house of Israel after those days"—the LORD's declaration. "I will put my teaching within them and write it on their hearts. I will be their God, and they will be my people. No longer will one teach his neighbor or his brother, saying, 'Know the Lord,' for they will all know me, from the least to the greatest of them"—this is the LORD's declaration. "For I will forgive their iniquity and never again remember their sin." (Jer 31:31–34)

The Lord emphasizes and then reemphasizes that this is *his* declaration. Only God has the power and authority to keep this promise; God alone is their hope. And one day, the Messiah from "the house of Israel" and "the house of Judah" would make this new covenant with his perfect obedience to the old covenant and the perfect sacrifice of his own blood (Luke 22:20; Rom 5:12–21), and the Lord's Spirit would come to fulfill this promise.

THE LORD IS THE SPIRIT

As Paul encourages the church in Corinth to rely on the Holy Spirit, he points back to the promise in Jeremiah 31. The promise-keeping God has sent his Spirit to them, just as he said. First promised to the Israelites of Jeremiah's day, this promise would be given to all God's people one day—and that day has come.

As those who believe in Christ, they received this promise. In fact, through Christ they, in some sense, embody that promise as Christ's body, the church. They are "Christ's letter, delivered by us, not written with ink but with the Spirit of the living God—not on tablets of stone [as in the days of Moses] but on tablets of human hearts" (2 Cor 3:3)

Now, God has always been triune. There was never a time when God was not Father, Son, and Holy Spirit, because God never changes (Num 23:19; Heb 13:8). But in

God's economy of redemption—the unveiling of his salvation given to us—he revealed himself as triune most clearly in the sending of the Son and the Holy Spirit. Historically speaking, he unveiled his triune nature in real time and space through a providential course of events; biblically speaking, he unveiled his triune nature through the unified witness of the Old Testament and New Testament. What Jeremiah 31 was pointing *forward to*—namely, the new covenant—is now fulfilled in the coming of the Son and Holy Spirit, which Paul explains by pointing *back to* here in 2 Corinthians. Because the triune God is the author of the entire story, it is no surprise that the Old Testament and New Testament—or perhaps more precisely, the old and new covenants in this context—exist in a mutually authoritative, reciprocal relationship. In sum, Paul cites the authority of God's promise spoken through Jeremiah in order to show that the promise was kept through the work of the Son and the Holy Spirit.

Jesus made the same type of interpretive move several times during his ministry. In John 5, for example, he tells the Jews:

You don't have [the Father's] word residing in you, because you don't believe the one he sent. You pore over the Scriptures because you think you have eternal life in them, and yet they testify about me.

But you are not willing to come to me so that you may have life. … How can you believe, since you accept glory from one another but don't seek the glory that comes from the only God? Do not think that I will accuse you to the Father. Your accuser is Moses, on whom you have set your hope. For if you believed Moses, you would believe me, because he wrote about me. But if you don't believe what he wrote, how will you believe my words? (John 5:38–40, 44–47)

Similarly, Jesus models this to his disciples on the road to Emmaus: "Beginning with Moses and all the Prophets, he interpreted for them the things concerning himself in all the Scriptures" (Luke 24:27). This is crucial to understanding Paul's point, because his argument for placing our confidence in the gospel is rooted in God keeping his promises. Moses, "the tablets," and prophets like Jeremiah were all pointing beyond themselves. They were pointing to the new covenant, secured in Christ's blood and applied in the Holy Spirit's indwelling. It is not as though Jesus came along because all the previous covenants and biblical figures surprisingly were not good enough; rather, the things of old were always pointing to him, and by extension to the eternal triune God who existed before them and stood beyond them. The sending of the Son was the plan A that the prior things were always moving toward; not a plan B emergency surgery to fix the problem.

The law was never meant to save, and now the fulfillment has come (2 Cor 3:7–9; Rom 8:1–4). Jesus kept the law perfectly, and salvation has been extended to all people by the Holy Spirit. The Corinthians, then, should not rely merely on the law as some still did, because "still today, whenever Moses is read, a veil lies over their hearts"; however, "whenever a person turns to the Lord, the veil is removed" (2 Cor 3:15–16). God's self-veiling in Exodus 32–34 was both an act of mercy and judgment on Moses and the people—mercy because he was still present among his sinful people; judgment because their sinfulness made them unable to see him.[26] And yet Paul tells them that now, they can turn to the Lord, unveiled, in mercy without judgment.

Now, who is this Lord they should turn to? In order to do full justice to the question, Paul cannot help but speak again in soaring language about the Holy Spirit:

> Now the Lord is the Spirit, and where the Spirit of the Lord is, there is freedom. We all, with unveiled faces, are looking as in a mirror at the glory of the Lord and are being transformed into the same image from glory to glory; this is from the Lord who is the Spirit. (2 Cor 3:17–18)

Moses, great as he was, was never able to see the Lord's glory with his own eyes (Exod 33:18–21), and yet the Holy Spirit, who himself is the Lord, has given us a clearer and deeper look at God's glory and the glory that awaits us in the new heavens and new earth. It is hard to fathom a more beautiful, majestic sight than looking upon the face of the almighty God of the universe, so it should knock the Corinthians (and us!) off our feet to think that this glorious Lord has revealed himself so clearly through the incarnation of the Son and the illumination of the Holy Spirit. The Lord himself, the Holy Spirit, transforms and renews us by turning our hearts from stone to flesh, forgiving our iniquities, and restoring our relationship with our creator. This promise-keeping triune God, Paul reminds them, has freed us from the curse of the law.

BEING TRANSFORMED

Today, we have the hindsight of a fully formed biblical canon. We can see from beginning to end; we know the score of the game before it is over. As with the Corinthians, we should use our hindsight to our advantage. We know God keeps his promises, because the Son and the Holy Spirit have come.

The Lord Jesus Christ has done everything needed to fulfill the law and free us from the curse, and the Holy Spirit has been poured out so we can walk in the freedom offered by the Lord who is the Spirit. "Such is the confidence we have through Christ before God. ... Since, then, we have such a hope, we act with great boldness" (2 Cor 3:4, 12).

A PRAYER

Father, we know that your Word is true and that you keep your promises. Help us to believe your Word and promises. In Jesus's name, by the Spirit we pray. Amen.

CHAPTER TWELVE

Triune Salvation
EPHESIANS 1:1-14

T hus far, we have continued to tie together the Old Testament and New Testament in our Trinitarian readings, showing that this is a canonical, whole-Bible argument and not merely relegated to the New Testament. The Trinity didn't begin in the coming of the Son and Holy Spirit, but rather was fully *revealed* by their fulfillments of Old Testament promises and patterns. In order to assert that Jesus and the Holy Spirit are fully God, a refrain emerges: only God can save, only God is worthy of worship, only God can keep the promises of God, and only God can reveal himself to us. If this is true—and the Old Testament is replete with these affirmations—then we are pressured to exalt and worship Jesus and the Holy Spirit because they say and do things we confess only God can do. This is a point worth reinforcing in our discussions of the Old Testament witness to the triune God, for this refrain about God's sovereignty and power is the foundation on which confessing the divinity of the Son and Spirit is built. As we consider the Trinitarian theology in Ephesians 1, it is worth reflecting on the swaths of Old Testament passages we have considered thus far about the nature and activity of God.

Though we have seen clear snapshots of Trinitarian theology throughout many biblical passages, the first chapter of Ephesians lays out perhaps the clearest Trinitarian vision of salvation, in particular the activity of the Trinitarian persons in salvation. In this one act of redemption, the three persons are unified active agents, exercising divine power. "Salvation belongs to the LORD," Psalm 3:8 tells us, and Ephesians 1 explains in explicit terms that this Lord is the triune God—Father, Son, and Holy Spirit.

TRIUNE SALVATION

As Paul does with many of his letters, he greets the church by stating his name and apostleship, followed by a type of blessing. In this case, he says, "Grace to you and peace from God our Father and the Lord Jesus Christ" (Eph 1:2).

It would make sense for Paul to say that grace and peace come from the Father. This is who God is—the one who promises grace and peace if we worship him. But as is so often the case, Jesus is included in this divine blessing as well. Paul cannot talk about divine blessing and worship without including the Lord Jesus Christ. If we think back to 1 Corinthians 8:6, we see this "new Shema" worship language—"one God, Father and ... one Lord, Jesus Christ"—that permeates these greetings.

The earliest Christians clearly recognized that whatever their reception of long-promised divine blessings looked like, it had a Trinitarian shape. Paul's final words in his second letter to the Corinthians—"The grace of the Lord Jesus Christ, and the love of God, and the fellowship of the Holy Spirit be with you all" (2 Cor 13:13)—have a similar structure and include the Holy Spirit, as does Peter's greeting in his first letter:

> To those chosen, living as exiles dispersed abroad in Pontus, Galatia, Cappadocia, Asia, and Bithynia, chosen according to the foreknowledge of God the Father, through the sanctifying work of the Spirit, to be obedient and to be sprinkled with the blood of Jesus Christ. (1 Pet 1:1b–2)

Though Paul doesn't include the Holy Spirit in his greeting the Ephesians, we will see that the Spirit is by no means forgotten or relegated to the sidelines. After the greeting, Paul launches into a beautiful, poetic portrait of the specific ways the Trinitarian persons secure and seal our redemption. Even though the three persons have distinct activities attributed to them here, we need not assume that there is some sort of bare hierarchy or varying levels of importance. All three persons are integral to our salvation—take one person away, and the whole thing falls apart. Again, salvation belongs to the Lord, and that *one* Lord in *three* persons. These three persons are fully and equally God, entirely one in will, power, and authority. To conclude otherwise would be to divide God into three parts, unnecessarily introducing potential change, division, or conflict among the persons. These types of small theological moves can turn into large errors. Ephesians 1 paints a stunning portrait of the unity of the Father, Son, and Holy Spirit.

Paul starts with the Father:

Blessed is the God and Father of our Lord Jesus Christ, who has blessed us with every spiritual blessing in the heavens in Christ. For he chose us in him, before the foundation of the world, to be holy and blameless in love before him. He predestined us to be adopted as sons through Jesus Christ for himself, according to the good pleasure of his will, to the praise of his glorious grace that he lavished on us in the Beloved One. (Eph 1:3–6)

The Father who gives all good and perfect gifts (Jas 1:17) has given us the greatest gift—access to all his riches as sons and daughters. It is fitting to speak about the Father as the one who wants to give an inheritance to his children. This does not mean that the Son and Holy Spirit have nothing to offer, or that they are simply bystanders. Instead, we see that the Father is, in some meaningful sense, a *father* to us. It is not an empty title but communicates something about who he is. The Father loved us so deeply, and his love overflowed so fully, that even in our sinfulness and rebellion—indeed, *before* it ever happened—he still longs to give us everything that is his.

Paul then moves on to the Son:

In him we have redemption through his blood, the forgiveness of our trespasses, according to the riches of his grace that he richly poured out on us with all wisdom and understanding. He made known to us the mystery of his will, according to his good pleasure that he purposed in Christ as a plan for the right time—to bring everything together in Christ, both things in heaven and things on earth in him. In him we have also received an inheritance, because we were predestined according to the plan of the one who works out everything in agreement with the purpose of his will, so that we who had already put our hope in Christ might bring praise to his glory. (Eph 1:7–12)

In Paul's articulation here, the unity between the Father and Son will redeem that which Adam and Eve broke. As we noted with the Father, "Son" is not a meaningless title. Because the Son is fully God, he lacks no power or authority whatsoever, even compared to the Father; however, it is nonetheless fitting for the Son to be the one who is sent and who, as the firstborn (Rom 8:29; Col 1:15), has a family inheritance to pass on from the Father to us. We are not required to say that the Son somehow has less authority or was waiting around for the Father to tell him what to do; instead, we should focus on the Father's love for us in sending the Son, and the Son's willingness to die for us. The Son put on flesh and bled for us not out of compulsion but out of overflowing divine love (John 10:18; Heb 12:2). Because of his power and authority as God, he is able to work in unity with the Father in revealing the divine mystery of the triune God's salvation.

Finally, he describes the Holy Spirit:

In him you also were sealed with the promised Holy Spirit when you heard the word of truth, the gospel of your salvation, and when you believed. The Holy Spirit is the down payment of our inheritance, until the redemption of the possession, to the praise of his glory. (Eph 1:13–14)

The Holy Spirit completes the plan of redemption by "sealing" our salvation, a "down payment" on our inheritance to secure our rights to it. This Holy Spirit was promised to come (Joel 2:28), and God keeps his promises. In our triune God's own good timing, he continues to deliver on every promise he has made, both now and into the future.

As we have discussed in other chapters, it is important to remember that the Holy Spirit is often portrayed as the one who completes the work of salvation. He may not always appear as prominently as the Father and Son in certain Gospel stories, for example, but he is always present in the most pivotal moments. Though his big crescendo at Pentecost occurs after the incarnation, the Holy Spirit is with Jesus long before Pentecost. Obviously, he is mentioned in the very first verses of the entire Bible at the beginning of all creation (Gen 1:2). But he is also present and active in Mary's conception (Matt 1:18), Jesus's baptism and temptation (Matt 3:13–17; 4:1), his miracle-working (for example, Matt 12:18), and his resurrection (Rom 8:11). Just as the Son was not waiting around for "something to do" before the incarnation (John 1:1–3), we must also say that the Holy Spirit was not waiting around for something to do before Pentecost. Because the Father, Son, and Holy Spirit are the one God who saves, there is never a time in which they are not in one accord and acting inseparably.

Of course, when we speak about the doctrine of the Trinity, we can only speak with the grammar given to us by the Bible. So where something might feel like a contradiction, we remember that God is perfect, and therefore there are no contradictions with him. We are with our finite minds trying to somehow comprehend just a little of the majesty of our triune God as revealed in Scripture.

REMEMBERING THE REFRAIN

It is easy to allow certain biblical truths to become white noise. We might say, "Yes, yes … only God can save. Of course, there are no rivals. We know God does not lie and keeps his promises." But as we reflect on Ephesians 1, we should pray to be awakened to the grace and peace of our triune God. We cannot save ourselves—God knows this. So God in his love and mercy does all the work for us. The Father moves toward us in love; in love, the Son lives the perfect obedient life that we cannot, culminating in his death, resurrection, and ascension to defeat sin and death; in love, the Holy Spirit is poured out on us to seal our salvation and to assure us that Jesus was telling the truth:

> I give them eternal life, and they will never perish. No one will snatch them out of my hand. My Father, who has given them to me, is greater than all. No one is able to snatch them out of the Father's hand. I and the Father are one. (John 10:28–30)

Salvation belongs to the Lord—Father, Son, and Holy Spirit.

A PRAYER

Father, our salvation is secure in the Son and Spirit. Grant us perseverance as we live in your grace and mercy. In Jesus's name, by the Spirit we pray. Amen.

CHAPTER THIRTEEN

Equality with God
PHILIPPIANS 2:5-11

I like to joke with friends that my greatest strength is my humility. Of course, this statement, if said seriously, would reek of irony. It's impossible to comment on your own humility without sounding arrogant. One way to know you're humble is not to brag about your humility. And though we shouldn't brag about our humility, we are called by God to pursue humility. The paradigm for this humility is the Son putting on flesh and dwelling among us.

The Bible describes the absolute power and transcendence of God in a way that, taken in isolation, could make us think that God is distant from us. And yet, we know that God has always been near to us in meaningful ways. When God created all things, we see that "the Spirit of God was hovering over the surface of the waters" (Gen 1:2). Later, when Adam and Eve sinned, they "heard the sound of the LORD God walking in the garden at the time of the evening breeze" (Gen 3:8). As we have discussed elsewhere, God was among the Israelites in a pillar of fire/cloud and the tabernacle—which literally means "the dwelling place"—as they wandered through the wilderness (Exod 13; 25–31; 35–40). Later, he was present in the temple (1 Kgs 8) and was present among his chosen servants (for example, Judg 3:10; 1 Sam 16:13).

Our passage in Philippians 2 is yet another example of God dwelling among us. Of course, as the omnipresent creator, he is ever present: "Can a person hide in secret places where I cannot see him? ... Do I not fill the heavens and the earth?" (Jer 23:24). Nonetheless, the biblical language about God coming down to us is not merely an empty concept—it is a declaration that our God is majestic, unrivaled, untouchable, and yet he draws near in love. When it comes to the incarnation, John says it plainly: "For God loved the world in this way: He gave his one and only Son, so that everyone who believes in him will not perish but have eternal life" (John 3:16).

HE EMPTIED HIMSELF

At first glance, Philippians 2:5–11 could be seen as a primarily moral passage; that is, the main point is following the example of Jesus and trying to be more humble. Now, we should not minimize the application, because Paul clearly has this type of application in mind. He says, "Adopt the same attitude as that of Christ Jesus" (Phil 2:5). But understanding that Jesus is God himself who has come to us, we should be floored by the sheer wonder of his mercy and grace.

As we have examined throughout this book, the mystery of the incarnation is the mystery of the eternal Son of God putting on flesh and dwelling among us. How could God, who is the creator of all things, thus wholly distinct from his creation, somehow step into and even, in some sense, become a part of creation? The simplest way that the church has worked out this idea is to say that Jesus Christ is two natures in one person—fully God and fully man. This is known as the "hypostatic union." Scripture talks about Jesus as God and as a human. He says and does things only God can do; and he says and does things all humans can do. He is both the God who saves and the man who is the perfectly obedient sacrifice. If he is not fully God, he cannot save; if he is not fully man, he cannot transfer salvation to fallen mankind. This is just who Jesus is: the God-man.

Paul starts here with Jesus's divinity: "... who, existing in the form of God, did not consider equality with God as something to be exploited" (Phil 2:6). Some translations say that Jesus did not "grasp at" equality with God, but the CSB's rendering offers helpful clarity: he did not *exploit* his divine nature. He never stopped being God—as though that is even possible for God to do!—but in his perfect humility, he was willing to "step down" and become human as well.

God promises to save his people; his longsuffering and covenant-keeping even in our rebellion shows that he will spare no resources to save us. In the mysterious plan of God, he demands a blood sacrifice. But because of his deep love, he is the one to shed his blood; because of his eternal perfection, he is able to be the perfect sacrifice who is not held in the grave by death's grip.

Next, Paul discusses Jesus's incarnation and humanity:

> Instead he emptied himself
>> by assuming the form of a servant,
>> taking on the likeness of humanity.
> And when he had come as a man,
>> he humbled himself by becoming obedient
>> to the point of death—
>> even to death on a cross. (Phil 2:7–8)

Paul emphasizes the absolute wonder that the transcendent, all-powerful, majestic, eternal Son of God put on flesh and dwelt among us. Similar to the "exploited" language above, we are not forced to misunderstand the statement that the Son "emptied himself." The New Testament shows Jesus exercising and claiming divine power throughout his life and ministry, so it would be a contradiction to claim that he put his divinity on the shelf in his incarnation. In fact, Paul tells us *how* he humbled himself: "by becoming obedient to the point of death, even to death on a cross" (Phil 2:8).

As the second person of the Trinity, Jesus is divine and thus subject to no one. He has all the power and authority of God because he is God. In the incarnation, he assumed a human nature to become obedient to the Father to undo the curse of the disobedient man, Adam: "For just as through one man's disobedience the many were made sinners, so also through the one man's obedience the many will be made righteous" (Rom 5:19).

Paul then switches back to exaltation language, though related to Jesus's human vocation:

> For this reason God highly exalted him
>> and gave him the name
>> that is above every name,

> so that at the name of Jesus
> every knee will bow—
> in heaven and on earth
> and under the earth—
> and every tongue will confess
> that Jesus Christ is Lord,
> to the glory of God the Father. (Phil 2:9–11)

As the eternal Son of God, he is already exalted to the highest of heights. However, the Son is exalted as the man who lived a perfect life full of grace and truth. His resurrection and ascension are the proof that he conquered sin and death and broke the chains of Adam's sin. In his perfect work as the God-man, he secured our salvation and guaranteed our future resurrection as "co-heirs with Christ" (Rom 8:17; 1 Cor 15).

ADOPTING THE ATTITUDE OF CHRIST

Paul says here that Jesus is God in all that it means to be God ("in the form of God"), but he chose not to exploit his divinity. Paul's point: we should be willing to sacrifice ourselves for the sake of others, even if it means not exploiting or grasping after the advantages *we possess*. Nowhere does Paul tell the Philippians to sell all their possessions or to renounce their "rights"; rather, Paul instructs them to be like Christ, who did not look out for his own interests even though he had every right to. As followers of Christ who walk in the Spirit, we become servants of all.

Of course, we cannot do this under our own power (and that is the point). God the Son stepped into human history and obeyed on our behalf. Now, through faith in Christ and by the power of the Holy Spirit, we are to walk in humility. We can never match a God-becoming-incarnate-level humility, but we can strive by the Holy Spirit to be humble in the lives he has given us.

A PRAYER

Father, we are unable to obey your word on our own. But you have given us everything we need in the obedience of your Son. Grant us humility to walk in his way. In Jesus's name, by the Spirit we pray. Amen.

CHAPTER FOURTEEN

The Firstborn Image
COLOSSIANS 1:15-20

Ivan the Terrible was a notoriously vicious king. The tsar of Russia from the sixteenth century, his most famous story of cruelty involves him murdering his oldest son and grandson—two generations of heirs to his throne—in a fit of rage. From his family to his people to his dealings with other nations, Ivan was ruthlessly cruel and self-absorbed.

Ivan is a notorious case, but not an isolated case. History is replete with kings whose thirst for power drove them to murder their own sons, if it meant that their power and authority would be preserved and unchallenged. This tendency for the abuse of power makes the story of the Father sending his Son that much more remarkable.

Jesus is called "the firstborn" here in Colossians 1, but the term's roots go back to the Old Testament. The term "firstborn" has two connotations in the Old Testament. The first is literal: the first-birthed child of a father. The second is more metaphorical or figurative: the child who has the rights and privilege to the father's wealth, even if they are not the one literally born first. These firstborn privileges can be taken away, as was the case with Reuben (Gen 35:23), or even stolen, in the case of Jacob and Esau (Gen 25:19–34).

Israel was given the privileged status as Yahweh's "firstborn" nation, which gives the word a corporate meaning too, based not on literal birth but on God's election and plan. In Psalm 89:27, God's covenant with King David includes an appointment to firstborn status—"I will make him my firstborn, greatest of the kings of the earth"—as well as a promise more generally to his throne. In the context of God's faithfulness to, and love for, his people, the "firstborn" language takes on a figurative meaning, as people and nations are chosen to advance God's purposes as he moves history toward final restoration (Rev 21–22). In every moment, God was drawing his people into his kingdom and offering grace in their missteps. Their inheritance was ultimately always from him (Eph 1:3–14).

In our passage from Colossians 1, Jesus is spoken of as the firstborn over all creation in relation to his inseparable work from the Father. Far from distant, ruthless tyrants, we see that God comes near to us through the sending of the Son. This love between the Father and Son is an eternal love that surpasses understanding and yet is modeled to us (John 17:24), and the Son's firstborn status indicates his unique status as the redeemer who brings us into the family and kingdom of God.

THE FIRSTBORN IMAGE

In this passage, Paul ties together the unity of the Father and the Son in salvation, in which the Father brings us into "the kingdom of his Son" by his blood. Of course, this kingdom is said to be the Father's in various places (Matt 6:10; 26:29), and yet the kingdom is described as the Son's kingdom here. One cannot ultimately talk about the kingdom of God without a reference to the Father and Son, for both are God. The Father saves us through and inseparably from the work of his Son.

Jesus "is the image of the invisible God, the firstborn over all creation" (Col 1:15). God is always present among us, and yet not even Moses was able to look directly at him (Exod 33:12–23). But in the incarnation, God's people were able to truly look God in the eyes, in the face of Jesus. One of his disciples, Philip, once asked, "Show us the Father."

Even after all the works Jesus had done and all the times Jesus had talked about the Father, Philip was still curious or perhaps still skeptical. But if he could *see* the Father, that would be "enough for the disciples." Jesus's response highlights the Trinitarian unity between the Father and Son:

> Jesus said to him, "Have I been among you all this time and you do not know me, Philip? The one who has seen me has seen the Father. How can you say, 'Show us the Father'? Don't you believe that I am in the Father and the Father is in me? The words I speak to you I do not speak on my own. The Father who lives in me does his works. Believe me that I am in the Father and the Father is in me. Otherwise, believe because of the works themselves. (John 14:9–11)

Notice that Jesus does not say, "One day, Philip—just wait until you die." Instead, he says that the Father they long to see, they see him in the flesh and bones of Jesus. This highlights the unity and distinction in the Trinity. The Father and Son are both God, both working inseparably and in one accord, yet they are not each other. Of course, the disciples did not fully understand this, but Jesus was intent on making the point. Here in Colossians 1, Paul summarizes the biblical story: God has always been present, but the incarnation of the Son made him visible in a way previously unthinkable.

The "firstborn" designation was at the center of the Trinitarian controversy in the early church. Just like describing Jesus as the "Son," the language of him as the "firstborn" brings to mind a type of subordination—that Jesus is somehow less than the Father. If he is some sort of child of the Father, then some have assumed that the Son is at the very least under the Father's authority, or perhaps even created by the Father. This potential subordination was central to early Trinitarian debates, and those early debates can help us see the Trinitarian dynamic of this passage.

Athanasius of Alexandria said that the idea of a divine hierarchy diminishing the Son's divinity misunderstands biblical analogies.[27] The Bible uses human analogy to explain what would be indescribable otherwise. Think of the Lord walking in the garden or reaching down his mighty right arm or bending his ear toward us (Gen 3:8; Ps 89:13; 116:2). Again, Scripture says that God is "spirit" and immaterial, so the idea that he has actual physical limbs would be a stretch. Not only that, but we instinctively know that these are analogies to help us understand God's presence and power. Since the Father is eternal and doesn't procreate biologically like humans do, then we have to understand that the Son has an eternal nature like his Father, and thus is somehow truly a Son and yet uncreated.

Even within biblical usage, "firstborn" does not always mean that someone was created. God has shown that he can providentially appoint someone to firstborn status as a way to move forward his plans of redemption. So, when we think about the firstborn designation for the Son in this passage, we need to consider the immediate context and broader biblical context. Immediately, we will see the clear divine language about the Son that is befitting of the eternal God, not a created being; relatedly, the broader biblical context helps us to see that a literal birth is not required for someone to have firstborn status. The incarnation includes a real human birth, in which the Son was really born as a real baby; however, this passage speaks about his eternal firstborn status, given that the context is about his rank above all creation, not his place within creation. This is reinforced as the passage continues.

> For everything was created by him,
>> in heaven and on earth,
>> the visible and the invisible,
>> whether thrones or dominions
>> or rulers or authorities—

all things have been created through him and
    for him.
He is before all things,
    and by him all things hold together. (Col 1:1–17)

As we have discussed in several chapters, the placement of Jesus on the creator side of the creator/creature divide is one of the clearest indications of his full divinity. Before the incarnation—in which he stepped into creation and put on flesh—he was in no way a creature, because "he is before all things" and "everything was created by him." In Romans 8:29, Paul draws on similar imagery, arguing that the Son was the firstborn in God's eternal decree. As the eternal firstborn Son, he stands above all because they were created by and for him.

Similar to Philippians 2:5–11, Paul started with language more proper to Jesus's divinity and then moved toward incarnation language. Now the language regarding his humanity starts:

He is also the head of the body, the church;
    he is the beginning,
    the firstborn from the dead,
    so that he might come to have
    first place in everything. (Col 1:18)

The "firstborn" designation comes through again, but this time in the context of his resurrection ("the firstborn from the dead"). In 1 Corinthians, Paul uses the term "firstfruits," which helps us understand his point here in Colossians:

> But as it is, Christ has been raised from the dead, the firstfruits of those who have fallen asleep. For since death came through a man, the resurrection of the dead also comes through a man. For just as in Adam all die, so also in Christ all will be made alive. But each in his own order: Christ, the first-fruits; afterward, at his coming, those who belong to Christ. (1 Cor 15:20–23)

Jesus's resurrection was a type of new birth for all of humanity, and his resurrection enables the resurrection of all who call on his name.

We are once again confronted with the beautiful reality of Jesus's divinity and humanity as Paul closes this miniature confession:

> For God was pleased to have
>   all his fullness dwell in him,
>   and through him to reconcile
>   everything to himself,
>   whether things on earth or things in heaven,
>   by making peace

through his blood, shed on the cross. (Col 1:19–20)

Jesus is the eternal Son who put on flesh. He is the God-man in whom "the fullness of God dwells," and he has reconciled all things through his incarnation, namely his "blood, shed on the cross." He is the creator and sustainer of all things whose obedience, death, and resurrection exalt him to the place of "head of the church."

LOOKING AT THE IMAGE

We do not have a king who is distant, vindictive, or power-hungry. When God says, "I AM WHO I AM" (Exod 3:14), he indicates that he is entirely self-sufficient, lacking nothing, with no rival. And yet he is still near to us, and he draws us into his kingdom.

Paul's confession about the centrality of Christ is certainly a statement about Christ, but it is also a broader Trinitarian confession, because the unity of the Father and Son (and the Holy Spirit) is the grammar of Christian confession. With Philip, we may be tempted at times to demand more from God. When we are suffering or even merely curious, we may ask for a sign or demand that God behave how we want. And yet, Jesus might say to us, "If you have seen me, you have seen the Father." We might hear him saying to us now through the Holy Spirit, "If you have read the Scriptures, you have seen me." We are able to see the person and work of that invisible God made visible in the words of Scripture. As Paul says elsewhere,

> All Scripture is inspired by God and is profitable for teaching, for rebuking, for correcting, for training in righteousness, so that the man of God may be complete, equipped for every good work. (2 Tim 3:16–17)

When we read the Scriptures, we are given what we need to worship our triune God as he has revealed himself. Our king acts only in righteousness, goodness, and truth, and we are the inheritors (Eph 1:3–14).

A PRAYER

Father, you graciously sent your Son to us. Thank you for granting us access to eternal life through his incarnation. In Jesus's name, by the Spirit we pray. Amen.

CHAPTER FIFTEEN

The Exact Imprint of His Nature
HEBREWS 1

Hebrews is a beautiful commentary on the Old Testament. Through various characters and stories, the author shows that the Son is the end goal of human history. In Hebrews 1, we are introduced to Jesus's superiority over the prophets and angels—God's messengers. These messengers serve as a foil for the author's argument about Jesus's divine nature and exalted humanity. When God speaks, the Son speaks.

God's speech is one of the core ways to describe God's activity in the world. When God created the heavens and the earth, he brought everything to order by speaking.

Genesis 1 uses the phrase "God said" ten times. Whether he is creating, bringing things to order, or giving commands to Adam and Eve, God does so by speaking. God's speech is powerful and has real-world effects. As he says through Isaiah,

> My word that comes from my mouth
>> will not return to me empty,
>> but it will accomplish what I please
>> and will prosper in what I send it to do.
>>> (Isa 55:11)

God does not always shout from the heavens to his people, rather he often speaks through chosen messengers.

Throughout the exodus account, for example, God speaks primarily through Moses, who then delivers those words to the Hebrews. Moses was the first in a long line of prophets through whom God would communicate to his people. This was God's consistent mode of communication, so much so that, "after the death of Moses the LORD's servant, the LORD spoke to Joshua son of Nun, Moses's assistant" (Josh 1:1). This mantle continued to be passed throughout the history of Israel, and much of the Old Testament is dedicated to God speaking through the prophets as his chosen vessels. When he spoke through these prophets, the words carried the very power and authority of God. As he says through Ezekiel, "But I, the

LORD, will speak whatever message I will speak, and it will be done. ... I will speak a message and bring it to pass" (Ezek 12:25).

God also at times spoke through angels—a word which literally means "messengers." These heavenly beings would function in similar ways to prophets, with the Lord speaking through them in particular moments. Many times the "angel of the Lord" delivered specific messages to chosen servants, like Abraham or Gideon (Gen 16:7–14; Judg 6:11–23). These messengers—whether prophets or angels—were God's primary means of communicating with his people. But, unsurprisingly, the incarnation of the Son changed things.

THE EXACT IMPRINT OF HIS NATURE

Hebrews 1 speaks clearly about the Son's divinity and humanity. The author moves seamlessly between saying that Jesus made the universe and atoned for our sins—without further explanation. It's as though this fact of the hypostatic union is common parlance among the earliest Christians.

The author of Hebrews starts the letter with the Old Testament. The audience is told that "long ago God spoke to our ancestors by the prophets at different times and in different ways" (Heb 1:1). In establishing the authority of the Son, the author starts with the authority of the prophets. Jesus similarly tells the Jews in particular that his authority and ministry is in continuity with their ancestors (Luke 24:44; John 5:46–47). If they believed the prophets, they should believe Jesus's words, because "in these last days, he has spoken to us by his Son" (Heb 1:2a). The divine authority of God's words was once mediated though the prophets but now comes through God himself in the person of the Son.

Jesus is not merely another prophet through whom God speaks; rather, "God has appointed him heir of all things and made the universe through him" (Heb 1:2b). As we think back to Colossians 1:15–20, we are reminded that the eternal Son is the firstborn heir of God's inheritance. We might say that this is a type of *eternal* appointment—tied to his divine nature and work—though there is likely an aspect of his humanity here as well in light of his exaltation to God's "right hand" (Heb 1:3a).[28] As the one through whom all things were made, his preexistence and divine power entail an authority that exceeds any mere prophet or messenger. In light of this, he is the ultimate and final prophet who has come to deliver God's address to his people as the eternal Son who is, as John 1:1–3 says, himself God's Word.

Further, Jesus "is the radiance of the glory of God and the exact imprint of his nature" who "upholds the universe by the word of his power" (Heb 1:3 ESV). If there was any question about Jesus's divine nature and power, the author of Hebrews clarifies it here. The Trinitarian implications are clear: the Son who made "purification for sins" and "sat down at the right hand of the Majesty on high" (Heb 1:3b) is truly man—our priest and sacrifice (Heb 4:14–16)—and yet we cannot overlook or discount his divine nature. The one who created and sustains creation stepped into that same creation to redeem it. The prophets are no longer needed, for God's Word himself, the eternal Son, has put on flesh and dwelt among us. When the Son speaks, God speaks (John 12:49).

Finally, the author turns to a comparison with the angels, God's heavenly messengers. He has established that the Son has come from heaven, so a question might then be raised, "What is the difference between the Son and the angels?" After all, angels are heavenly messengers sent by God, but Jesus is "much superior to angels as the name he has inherited is more excellent than theirs" (Heb 1:4). Here we again see the reference to Jesus's exalted humanity as the one who sits at the right hand of God. Jesus's superiority to the angels is both a divine and human claim. He is obviously greater as God, for angels are still creatures; and he is above the angels according to his humanity—the true image of God as the perfect man.

The author of Hebrews shows the Son's superiority by drawing on several Old Testament texts in Hebrews

1:5–14. First, he cites Psalm 2:7 and 2 Samuel 7:14 as well as 1 Chronicles 17:13 to show that angels are never called "Son":

> For to which of the angels did he ever say,
>> You are my Son;
>> today I have become your Father,
>> or again,
> I will be his Father,
>> and he will be my Son?

Next, referring to Deuteronomy 32:43[29] and Psalm 97:7, he says that the angels worship the Son and are merely his servants:

> Again, when he brings his firstborn into the world, he says,
> And let all God's angels worship him.
> And about the angels he says:
> He makes his angels winds,
>> and his servants a fiery flame.

Psalm 45:6–7 is next, with the author insinuating that this passage is ultimately a type of conversation between the Father and Son, in which the Father calls the Son "God."[30]

> But [the Father says] to the Son:
> Your throne, God,

is forever and ever,
and the scepter of your kingdom
is a scepter of justice.
You have loved righteousness
and hated lawlessness;
this is why God, your God,
has anointed you
with the oil of joy
beyond your companions.

He then quotes Psalm 102:25–27 as another word from the Father to the Son, reiterating the Son's role as creator of the heavens:

And [the Father says]:
In the beginning, Lord,
you established the earth,
and the heavens are the works of your hands;
they will perish, but you remain.
They will all wear out like clothing;
you will roll them up like a cloak,
and they will be changed like clothing.
But you are the same,
and your years will never end.

Finally, quoting Psalm 110:1, he speaks of the Son's exaltation to God's right hand—a place angels, who are merely servants, have never been invited to:

Now to which of the angels has he ever said:
Sit at my right hand
    until I make your enemies your footstool?
Are they not all ministering spirits sent out to serve
    those who are going to inherit salvation?

In all these Old Testament citations, the author of Hebrews uses the authority of the Old Testament as a way to reinforce the prologue.

In sum, the angels cannot compete with the Son's superiority—he is the Son who created all things and has been exalted in his perfect humanity. The angels are simply "ministering spirits sent out" as servants of the Lord (Heb 1:14). In every respect—divine and human—the Son is superior. He leaves no doubt that the Son is not a creaturely messenger, but rather the divine Son who is worthy of worship and who has redeemed God's image-bearers.

THE SUPERIOR SON

Hebrews 1 lifts our eyes to the Son who is superior to angels and prophets alike. Whereas angels and prophets are servants of the Lord, he is the Lord whom they serve. God has spoken through the Son—his word is our authority, his work our salvation.

The prophets were chosen men with significant ministries, but they too were instruments of our triune God.

As Peter tells us, "No prophecy ever came by the will of man; instead, men spoke from God as they were carried along by the Holy Spirit" (2 Pet 1:21). When the prophets spoke, the Holy Spirit spoke; when the Holy Spirit spoke, God spoke. This Trinitarian dynamic in the text helps order our attention and ultimately our worship.

A PRAYER

Father, your Son is above all things and yet has come to us. Grant us ears to hear the words of the Son and Spirit. In Jesus's name, by the Spirit we pray. Amen.

CHAPTER SIXTEEN

Triune Worship
REVELATION 1:4-5; 4-5

When people think about the book of Revelation, they often picture the world literally on fire. However, Revelation is not primarily a book about destruction, meteorites, world wars, and death. There are elements of these things, for sure, but it is primarily about hope, encouragement, and an unimaginably joyful eternity with our triune God. It is not about escaping earth up to heaven but about heaven coming down to earth. It is not about how the world ends but about how the world is remade and restored to perfect relationship with our triune God (Rev 21–22).

Revelation is a vision of heaven that resembles God's prophets in the Old Testament, who were given rare access to the very throne room of God himself. Perhaps the most famous is Isaiah's vision:

> In the year that King Uzziah died, I saw the Lord seated on a high and lofty throne, and the hem of his robe filled the temple. Seraphim were standing above him; they each had six wings: with two they covered their faces, with two they covered their feet, and with two they flew. And one called to another:
>
> Holy, holy, holy is the LORD of Armies;
> his glory fills the whole earth. (Isa 6:1–3)

Isaiah's vision is similar to John's in Revelation. He is granted access to the throne room; he sees the Lord seated on a throne, and he sees a magnitude of remarkable creatures that sound straight out of fairy tales. Ezekiel likewise has a similar vision:

> Something like a throne with the appearance of lapis lazuli was above the expanse over their heads. On the throne, high above, was someone who looked like a human. From what seemed to be his waist up, I saw a gleam like amber, with what looked like fire enclosing it all around. From what seemed

to be his waist down, I also saw what looked like fire. There was a brilliant light all around him. The appearance of the brilliant light all around was like that of a rainbow in a cloud on a rainy day. This was the appearance of the likeness of the Lord's glory. When I saw it, I fell facedown and heard a voice speaking. (Ezek 1:26–28)

Similar to both Isaiah and John, Ezekiel sees a throne and seems to have trouble describing exactly what he is seeing, saying that what he sees is *like* this or *like* that.

John appears to be a prophet in line with those who have come before him. Chosen by the Lord to see a glimpse into heaven, John is told to write down what he sees and report back to his people. Throughout Revelation, John quotes the prophets in nearly every sentence, because their visions help him describe the indescribable and because they act as an authority for the authenticity of his vision. John's vision stands out from the rest, however, because his has the most clearly Trinitarian portrait.

TRIUNE WORSHIP

Many recognize that Revelation exalts Jesus without reservation. Even some who are skeptical of a Trinitarian reading of Scripture recognize that one must deal with the divine language directed at Jesus in the book.[31] John's vision is a vision of the triune God.

The Trinitarian language starts in the introduction. After a brief prologue, John turns to a greeting to the seven churches of Asia minor. Much like we see in the greetings we have noted in Paul and Peter, John's greeting is in the form of a doxology:

> To the seven churches in Asia. Grace and peace to you from the one who is, who was, and who is to come, and from the seven spirits before his throne, and from Jesus Christ, the faithful witness, the first-born from the dead and the ruler of the kings of the earth. To him who loves us and has set us free from our sins by his blood. (Rev 1:4–5a)

Because Revelation is a type of apocalyptic literature, much of John's language uses imagery, symbols, and numbers to describe his vision. So, as we move forward, we will seek to clarify the Trinitarian picture he paints by highlighting how he describes or names the Trinitarian persons.

First, we have the Father: "the one who is, who was, and who is to come." This description speaks to the Father's eternality. He is the past, present, and future; put another way, he is outside of time because he created it. He is not constrained by history's forward-ticking clock.

This is almost certainly a play on God's eternal name in Exodus 3:14: "I AM WHO I AM."

Next, he mentions the Holy Spirit: "the seven spirits before his throne." Again, John often uses imagery, symbols, and numbers to make his claims. The number seven, for example, is often viewed in Scripture as the number of completion or perfection, most notably when seven is associated with the completion of God's "very good" creation (Gen 1). Throughout Revelation, John uses the number to indicate perfection or completion in numerous ways—seven spirits, seven churches, seven stars, seven lamps, seven angels, seven cycles of judgment, and so on. The seven spirits, however, are worshiped in a doxology.

Finally, he mentions Jesus Christ by name. In particular, he highlights his human exaltation as the one who died and raised. His divinity, however, is implicit in the fact that he is included in this doxology, which again is a type of worship language. One of the most basic rules for worship in the Bible is this: "I am the LORD your God, who brought you out of the land of Egypt, out of the place of slavery. Do not have other gods besides me" (Exod 20:2–3). In a book so concerned with true and false worship, John would not toss angels or spirits or even Jesus into a doxology unless they belonged there.

Notice the interchangeability of divine titles and descriptions in Revelation. For example, Revelation teaches that the Father and Jesus are one—they are both called "the First and the Last" or "Alpha and Omega" (Rev 1:8; 2:8; 22:13). Similarly, in the letters to the churches, each letter begins and ends with Jesus speaking and the Holy Spirit speaking (Rev 2–3).

In this greeting, then, John highlights both the unity and distinction of the persons. This vision of the triune God is dependent upon the unified work of the Father, Son, and Holy Spirit. They collectively provide this vision to John, and he beautifully and poetically makes that point from the start.

The other most striking Trinitarian picture in Revelation is John's vision of the glorious divine throne room. These scenes are packed full of beautiful and strange language, so we will simply look at a couple of excerpts:

> After this I looked, and there in heaven was an open door. The first voice that I had heard speaking to me like a trumpet said, "Come up here, and I will show you what must take place after this." Immediately I was in the Spirit, and there was a throne in heaven and someone was seated on it. (Rev 4:1–2)

The one seated on the throne is said later to be the "Lord God, the Almighty, who was, who is, and who is to come" (Rev 4:8). So we see someone seated on the throne, perhaps the Father in this instance, and he is rightly worshiped by those around the throne. As our gaze is transfixed on the stunning language describing the throne, we should not overlook the work of the Holy Spirit here. He is the one who, throughout the book, allows John to see his visions. He brings John into the vision to begin with (Rev 1:10) and guides him through the visionary journey (Rev 4:2; 17:3; 21:10). This being "in the Spirit" and "carried away by the Spirit" seems to be the way John receives this prophetic revelation, for he is commanded to "write down everything" he sees (Rev 1:11). Similar prophetic inspiration is found, for example, in Ezekiel 3:12 and 11:24. Peter's statement that God spoke through the prophets, by way of the Holy Spirit, to confess the knowledge of Christ comes to mind here as well (2 Pet 1:21). In short, John is unable to hear or see the divine message without the power and illumination of the Holy Spirit.

The next major scene occurs in Revelation 5. The scene is similar—the Almighty is worshiped on his throne by all of creation—but the praise is extended to Jesus as well:

They said with a loud voice,
Worthy is the Lamb who was slaughtered
   to receive power and riches

> and wisdom and strength
> and honor and glory and blessing!
> I heard every creature in heaven, on earth, under
> the earth, on the sea, and everything in them say,
> Blessing and honor and glory and power
> be to the one seated on the throne,
> and to the Lamb, forever and ever!

This eruption of worship is brought about by Jesus, "the Lamb," exercising unique power to open the scroll. Not only that, but Jesus is portrayed as "standing in the midst of the throne" with the "seven spirits" as his eyes (Rev 5:6). Two things are worth noting here.

First, Jesus is standing "in the midst of the throne" and receiving worship from all of creation. Put simply, he is sharing the throne with the Father without any sense of impropriety. No one tells Jesus to move aside; no one rebukes him for sharing in the praise that would seemingly be reserved for the Father alone. No, he belongs on the creator side of the creaturely hymns—he is as worthy of divine worship as the Father.

Second, the seven spirits make another appearance. This seems to be an allusion to Zechariah 4:6–10, where the "sevens spirits of God" are sent to be God's eyes on earth. This language of God's eyes having an all-encompassing gaze can also be compared to passages such as

Proverbs 15:3: "The eyes of the LORD are everywhere, observing the wicked and the good." In Isaiah 11:2 in the Septuagint—the Greek translation of the Hebrew Bible that many biblical authors cite—there is a sevenfold description of the gifts and activities of the Lord's Spirit. The Holy Spirit, then, is included in the doxology, speaks authoritatively with Jesus, brings divine revelation, allows John access to the divine throne room, and is portrayed as coming from the throne as Jesus's eyes aimed at creation. It seems we are left with the unavoidable conclusion that John creatively but clearly depicts the Holy Spirit as equally divine alongside the Father and Son.

Revelation, the capstone of the entire biblical canon, offers a beautiful vision of the triune God. In a book centered on worship of the breathtaking glory of our enthroned Almighty God, John describes the Trinitarian persons at every turn, seemingly unable to describe what he sees without mention of the Father, Son, and Holy Spirit.

WORSHIPING THROUGH THE VISION

John's vision is certainly perplexing at times, but the main point is clear: our triune God is worthy of worship. In fact, to worship God ultimately is to worship Father, Son, and Holy Spirit. The Son and Holy Spirit continue to speak to us. We are called to see the splendor of our triune God through the vision of John and to long for the new creation to come.

A PRAYER

Father, you are making all things new with and through your Son and Spirit. Grant us the vision to worship with all of creation as we await the Son's return. In Jesus's name, by the Spirit we pray. Amen.

CHAPTER SEVENTEEN

Three Rules for Reading Trinitarianly

The incarnation of the Son changed everything. And for two millennia, Christians have argued that the Scriptures fit together most clearly in light of the incarnation. For example, Irenaeus of Lyons, a second-century bishop who claimed to be taught by a disciple of the apostle John, shows us that the assumption of a unified scriptural witness was already commonplace among the earliest Christian communities.

In his work called *Against Heresies*, he battled heretical groups who claimed that the four Gospels weren't sufficient for understanding Jesus's teachings. Irenaeus, however, claimed that the heretics' interpretations contradicted

Scripture. Scripture, he said, is like a mosaic of precious jewels that make the image of a beautiful king. But because these false teachers fail to see how the Scriptures fit together, their interpretations turn the beautiful mosaic of the king into a poorly produced image of a dog or fox.[32]

Irenaeus's argument that Scripture is a unified story about the King is rooted in Scripture's own claims. Throughout this book, we have looked at numerous biblical texts that reveal the triune God and draw together Scripture's unified witness to him. As we conclude, here are three key rules for reading Scripture in light of the Trinity.

1. CHRIST IS AT THE CENTER

In Luke 24, the disciples find Jesus's tomb empty. Although they remembered that he had predicted his own death and resurrection, they were nonetheless shell-shocked by the whole ordeal. As two of them walked to the town of Emmaus, Jesus began to walk alongside them. To help them understand the events of the crucifixion and resurrection, he taught them about himself: "Beginning with Moses and all the Prophets, he interpreted for them the things concerning himself in all the Scriptures" (Luke 24:27). Though they were unable to recognize him until much later, they nonetheless reflected, "Weren't our hearts burning within us while he was talking with us on the road and explaining the Scriptures to us?" (Luke 24:32).

Later, he taught them once again that "'everything written about me in the Law of Moses, the Prophets, and the Psalms must be fulfilled.' Then he opened their minds to understand the Scriptures" (Luke 24:44–45). Even before his crucifixion, he began preparing his disciples and adversaries that this was key to understanding him and his ministry:

> For if you believed Moses, you would believe me, because he wrote about me. But if you don't believe what he wrote, how will you believe my words? (John 5:46–47)

> Your father Abraham rejoiced to see my day; he saw it and was glad. (John 8:56)

Time and time again, Jesus teaches them (and us) that the Scriptures are a unified story centered on him. One cannot understand the Old Testament without him; one cannot understand him without the Old Testament.

The New Testament authors understood this well and sought to understand the christological depth of the Scriptures. It should be no surprise, then, that these authors rely heavily on Old Testament citations and themes. They were simply following their teacher's model: searching the Scriptures to understand how it spoke about him.

As we read the Scriptures, our default setting should be christological; we should constantly be asking, how does it speak about him? We read trinitarianly when we read christologically because that same God is the God who put on flesh and dwelt among us. The key to the unity of Scripture is the mystery of the Trinity in the incarnation of the Son.

2. THE SPIRIT GIVES UNDERSTANDING

Similarly, reading trinitarianly includes reading with and under the guidance of the Holy Spirit. Paul puts it this way:

> For to this day, at the reading of the old covenant, the same veil remains; it is not lifted, because it is set aside only in Christ. Yet still today, whenever Moses is read, a veil lies over their hearts, but whenever a person turns to the Lord, the veil is removed. Now the Lord is the Spirit, and where the Spirit of the Lord is, there is freedom. (2 Cor 3:14–17)

In the gospel, the Holy Spirit sets us free from bondage to sin and enables us to walk freely in the grace of Christ (Rom 8). As Spirit-led readers of Scripture, we are able to understand, albeit imperfectly, the mysteries of the triune God's self-revelation (1 Cor 2). This was Jesus's promise, when he told his disciples, "But the Counselor, the Holy Spirit, whom the Father will send in my name, will teach you all things and remind you of everything I have told you" (John 14:26).

Paul tells us here in 2 Corinthians that the gospel lifts the "veil over our hearts" because we are able to see the unified witness of Scripture to the triune God. Without the Holy Spirit, we are unable to recognize Jesus's words in Luke 24: that the Old Testament speaks about him and points forward to his day. However, with the Holy Spirit's unveiling of our hearts, our hearts now "burn within us" as the Son speaks to us in the Scriptures from Genesis to Revelation.

And we are not merely readers of Scripture; Scripture reads *us*. Paul says elsewhere,

> The sacred Scriptures ... are able to give you wisdom for salvation through faith in Christ Jesus. All Scripture is inspired by God and is profitable for teaching, for rebuking, for correcting, for training in righteousness, so that the man of God may be complete, equipped for every good work. (2 Tim 3:15–17)

Don't overlook this point: to read trinitarianly is to read with the unveiled heart of faith and to walk in the freedom of the gospel by the power of the Holy Spirit.

3. THE TRINITY IS BIBLICAL GRAMMAR

The Trinity is the Christian doctrine of God. We discussed some basic Trinitarian categories at the beginning of this book that act as a type of interpretive grammar: nature, relations, inseparable operations, and the hypostatic union. Each category contributes to the whole, so that we can speak rightly about the triune God as he has revealed himself in Scripture.

Though we cannot cite these words with a mere chapter-and-verse quotation, these words are useful grammatical boundaries that help us make sense of the wide array of biblical statements about the Father, Son, and Holy Spirit. This grammar is summed up nicely in the *Gloria Patri*, a Christian doxology that dates to the second century or earlier:

> Glory be to the Father,
>> and to the Son, and to the Holy Spirit,
>> as it was in the beginning,
>> is now, and ever shall be,
>> world without end. Amen.

There is a beautiful simplicity to this doxology. Glory to the Father, Son, and Holy Spirit—the one triune God. We owe him our praise forever and ever. When we see the Father, Son, or Holy Spirit in Scripture, we see the triune God who is the I AM, the God of Israel, the one whose name is the foundation for our confession of faith and our baptism into the family of God.

A PRAYER

The grace of the Lord Jesus Christ, and the love of God, and the fellowship of the Holy Spirit be with you all. (2 Cor 13:14 ESV)

Acknowledgments

While writing my dissertation on the Trinity in the book of Revelation, I dreamed of someday writing a book on the Trinity and the Bible that would be more accessible for pastors, students, and laypeople. Thanks to the encouragement and support of Todd Hains, Jesse Myers, and the rest of the Lexham crew, that dream came to life in this book.

I am forever indebted to my wonderful wife, Christa, whose steadfast faith and co-laboring makes me a better man and inspires my walk with the triune God. Our life together with our three girls is my greatest earthly treasure.

I have the privilege of teaching on the Trinity, church history, and hermeneutics to hundreds of students every year at Cedarville University. The content of this book is largely birthed out of my ministry to them. I absolutely love teaching, and I pray that my joy for teaching them has bled over into this book.

Finally, I owe a special thanks to Trevin Wax, Matthew Bennett, Steve Bezner, Matthew Capps, Jeff Manning, and Michael Cooper for offering pastoral feedback on an early version of the manuscript. Their many insights made the book better. Thanks also to Cody Barnhart for his help with indexing the manuscript.

Recommended Reading

Irenaeus of Lyons. *On the Apostolic Preaching*. Translated by
John Behr. Popular Patristics Series. Crestwood, NY: St.
Vladimir's Seminary Press, 1997.

Athanasius of Alexandria. *On the Incarnation*. Translated by John
Behr. Popular Patristics Series. Yonkers, NY: St. Vladimir's
Seminary Press, 2011.

Basil the Great. *On the Holy Spirit*. Translated by David Anderson.
Popular Patristics Series. Crestwood, NY: St. Vladimir's
Seminary Press, 1980.

Gregory of Nazianzus. *On God and Christ: The Five Theological
Orations and Two Letters to Cledonius*. Translated by
Frederick Williams and Lionel Wickham. Popular Patristics
Series. Crestwood, NY: St. Vladimir's Seminary Press, 2002.

Cyril of Alexandria. *On the Unity of Christ*. Translated by John
Anthony McGuckin. Popular Patristics Series. Crestwood,
NY: St. Vladimir's Seminary Press, 1995.

Martin Luther. *The Last Words of David* (1543). In *Luther's Works*,
vol. 15, ed. Jaroslav Pelikan, pages 267–352. St. Louis:
Concordia, 1972.

John Gill. *Complete Body of Practical and Doctrinal Divinity*. Philadelphia: Delaplaine and Hellings, 1810. Available online at monergism.com/thethreshold/sdg/gill/A_Body_of_Doctrinal_Divinity_-_John_Gill.pdf.

Fred Sanders. *The Deep Things of God: How the Trinity Changes Everything*. 2nd ed. Wheaton, IL: Crossway, 2017.

R. B. Jamieson and Tyler R. Wittman. *Biblical Reasoning: Christological and Trinitarian Rules for Exegesis*. Grand Rapids: Baker Academic, 2022.

Scott R. Swain. *The Trinity: An Introduction*. Wheaton, IL: Crossway, 2020.

Works Cited

ANCIENT

Athanasius of Alexandria. *Against the Arians.* English translations
    consulted: *The Nicene and Post-Nicene Fathers,* Volume 4.
    Edited by Philip Schaff and Henry Wace. Translated by
    John Henry Newman and Archibald T. Robertson. New
    York: Christian Literature, 1892.

———. *Four Discourses Against the Arians.* Edited and Translated
    by Henry Bettenson. In *The Early Christian Fathers: A
    Selection from the Writings of the Fathers from St. Clement to
    St. Athanasius.* London: Oxford University Press, 1956.

———. *On the Incarnation.* English translation consulted: Saint
    Athanasius. *On the Incarnation.* Translated by John Behr.
    Popular Patristics Series. Yonkers, NY: St. Vladimir's
    Seminary Press, 2011.

Augustine of Hippo. *Lessons of the New Testament.* English
    translation consulted: *The Nicene and Post-Nicene Fathers,*
    Volume 6. Edited by Philip Schaff. Translated by R. G.
    MacMullen. Buffalo, NY: Christian Literature, 1888.

Basil of Caesarea. *On the Holy Spirit*. English translation consulted: St Basil the Great. *On the Holy Spirit*. Translated by David Anderson. Popular Patristics Series. Crestwood, NY: St. Vladimir's Seminary Press, 1980.

Gregory of Nazianzus. *Orations*. English translation consulted: St Gregory of Nazianzus. *On God and Christ: The Five Theological Orations and Two Letters to Cledonius*. Translated by Frederick Williams and Lionel Wickham. Popular Patristics Series. Crestwood, NY: St. Vladimir's Seminary Press, 2002.

Gregory of Nyssa. *Against Eunomius*. English translation consulted: Gregory of Nyssa. Contra Eunomium *III: An English Translation with Commentary and Supporting Studies*. Edited by Johan Leemans and Matthieu Cassin. Vigiliae Christianae Supplements 124. Leiden: Brill, 2014.

_____. *On Not Three Gods*. English translation consulted: *The Nicene and Post-Nicene Fathers*, Volume 5. Edited by Philip Schaff and Henry Wace. Translated by H.A. Wilson. Buffalo, NY: Christian Literature, 1893.

Hilary of Poitiers, *On the Trinity*. English translation consulted: St. Hilary of Poitiers. *The Trinity*. Translated by Stephen McKenna. The Fathers of the Church. Washington, D.C.; The Catholic University of America Press, 1954.

Irenaeus of Lyons. *Against the Heresies*. English translation consulted: *The Ante-Nicene Fathers*, Volume 1. Edited by Alexander Roberts, James Donaldson, and A. Cleveland Coxe. Translated Alexander Roberts and William Rambaut. New York: Christian Literature, 1885.

_____. *On the Apostolic Preaching*. English translation consulted: St. Irenaeus of Lyons, *On the Apostolic Preaching*. Translated

by John Behr. Popular Patristics Series. Crestwood, NY: St.
    Vladimir's Seminary Press, 1997.

John Chrysostom, *Homilies on John.* English translation
    consulted: *The Nicene and Post-Nicene Fathers,* volume
    14. Edited by Philip Schaff. Translated by Charles Marriott.
    Buffalo, NY: Christian Literature, 1889.

Luther, Martin. "That in Christ There Are Two Natures, United
    in Such a Way That Christ Is One Person" (1540). English
    translation consulted: *Luther's Works*, vol. 73. Translated by
    Jeffrey G. Silcock. St. Louis: Concordia Publishing House,
    2020.

Origen of Alexandria. *On First Principles.* English translation
    consulted: Origen. *On First Principles*, Volume 1. Edited
    and Translated by John Behr. Oxford Early Christian Texts.
    Oxford: Oxford University Press, 2017.

MODERN

Bauckham, Richard. *The Theology of the Book of Revelation.*
    Cambridge: Cambridge University Press, 1993.

Dunn, James D. G. *Did the First Christians Worship Jesus?: The New
    Testament Evidence.* Louisville: Westminster John Knox,
    2010.

Garland, David E. *2 Corinthians.* Christian Standard Commentary.
    Nashville: Holman, 2021.

Hurtado, Larry W. *Lord Jesus Christ: Devotion to Jesus in Earliest
    Christianity.* Grand Rapids: Eerdmans, 2003.

Jamieson, R. B. *The Paradox of Sonship: Christology in the Epistle to
    the Hebrews.* Studies in Christian Doctrine and Scripture.
    Downers Grove, IL: IVP Academic, 2021.

Kreeft, Peter and Ronald Tacelli. *Handbook of Christian Apologetics: Hundreds of Answers to Crucial Questions*. Downers Grove: IVP, 1994.

Lemesurier, Peter. *The Unknown Nostradamus: 500th Anniversary Biography*. London: John Hunt Publishing, 2003.

Lewis, C. S. *Mere Christianity*. London: William Collins, 1952.

Pierce, Madison N. *Divine Discourse in the Epistle to the Hebrews: The Recontextualization of Spoken Quotations of Scripture*. Society for New Testament Studies 178. Cambridge: Cambridge University Press, 2020.

Rowe, C. Kavin. "Biblical Pressure and Trinitarian Hermeneutics." *Pro Ecclesia* 11, no. 3 (2002): 295–312.

Sanders, Fred and Scott R. Swain. "Introduction." In *Retrieving Eternal Generation*, edited by Sanders and Swain. Grand Rapids: Zondervan Academic, 2017.

Smith, Brandon D. "What Christ Does, God Does: Surveying Recent Scholarship on Christological Monotheism." *Currents in Biblical Research* 17, no. 2 (2019): 184–208.

Vidu, Adonis. *The Same God Who Works All Things: Inseparable Operations in Trinitarian Theology*. Grand Rapids: Eerdmans, 2021.

Weinandy, Thomas G. *Jesus Becoming Jesus: A Theological Interpretation of the Synoptic Gospels*. Washington, D.C.; The Catholic University of America Press, 2018.

Endnotes

1 As Adonis Vidu, *The Same God Who Works All Things: Insepara-ble Operations in Trinitarian Theology* (Grand Rapids: Eerdmans, 2021), 95 says plainly: Trinitarian theology is "a gradual purifica-tion of our speech about God, by stipulating grammatical rules rather than shining the light of comprehension on transcendent realities."

2 Martin Luther, "That in Christ There Are Two Natures, United in Such a Way That Christ Is One Person" (1540), *Luther Works* 73:259. Here we could say that "the sense" is no less than the theological interpretation of the biblical narrative, whereas the "the words" are no more than twisting God's words out of context.

3 I owe this phrasing to Fred Sanders and Scott R. Swain, "Intro-duction," in *Retrieving Eternal Generation*, ed. Sanders and Swain (Grand Rapids: Zondervan Academic, 2017), 17.

4 These four principles are by no means exhaustive but are imme-diately helpful for our purposes in this book.

5 For a survey of the backgrounds and views of Jesus's divinity in the first century, see Brandon D. Smith, "What Christ Does, God Does: Surveying Recent Scholarship on Christological Mono-theism," *Currents in Biblical Research* 17, no. 2 (2019): 184–208.

6   See, for example, Irenaeus of Lyons, *Against Heresies* 1.8.1–1.9.4; and his *On the Apostolic Preaching* 6.

7   From "The Great Litany" in the Book of Common Prayer.

8   C. S. Lewis, *Mere Christianity* (London: William Collins, 1952), 54–56. Peter Kreeft and Ronald Tacelli, have famously argued that "legend" should be a fourth category. See *Handbook of Christian Apologetics: Hundreds of Answers to Crucial Questions* (Downers Grove, IL: IVP, 1994).

9   To be clear, Jesus did not become divine nor did he obtain divine power at his baptism. He is the eternal Son of God who existed before creation itself (for example, Matt 1:18–25; John 1:1–14; John 17:5; Phil 2:5–11; Col 1:15–20), and so his "ministry" is in a sense eternal, not confined to his time walking in or near Galilee and Judea.

10 For the idea of "biblical pressures," see C. Kavin Rowe, "Biblical Pressure and Trinitarian Hermeneutics," *Pro Ecclesia* 11, no. 3 (2002): 295–312.

11 Thomas G. Weinandy, *Jesus Becoming Jesus: A Theological Interpretation of the Synoptic Gospels* (Washington, D.C.: The Catholic University of America Press, 2018), 441.

12 *Lessons of the New Testament* 2.

13 Hilary of Poitiers, *On the Trinity* 2.1. English translation from St. Hilary of Poitiers, *The Trinity*, trans. Stephen McKenna (Washington, D.C.: The Catholic University of America Press, 1954).

14 The biblical idea of a creator/creature distinction became an important point in early Trinitarian debates. See, for example, Athanasius of Alexandria, *Against the Arians* 1.14–15.

15 Gregory of Nazianzus, *Oration* 28.17. English translation from St. Gregory of Nazianzus, *On God and Christ: The Five Theological Orations and Two Letters to Cledonius*, trans. Frederick Williams and Lionel Wickham, Popular Patristics Series (Crestwood, NY: St. Vladimir's Seminary Press, 2002).

16 Richard Bauckham, *The Theology of the Book of Revelation* (Cambridge: Cambridge University Press, 1993), 63.

17 Athanasius of Alexandria, *Against the Arians* 2.36. English translation from Athanasius, *Four Discourses Against the Arians*, ed. and trans. Henry Bettenson, in *The Early Christian Fathers: A Selection from the Writings of the Fathers from St. Clement to St. Athanasius* (London: Oxford University Press, 1956), 392.

18 John Chrysostom, *Homilies on John* 38.3 emphasizes that the Jews both understood that Jesus was claiming to be God and that he was not backing down from the claim.

19 *Against Eunomius* 3.4.33–35. English translation from Gregory of Nyssa, Contra Eunomium *III: An English Translation with Commentary and Supporting Studies*, ed. Johan Leemans and Matthieu Cassin, Vigiliae Christianae Supplements 124 (Leiden: Brill, 2014).

20 *On Not Three Gods* 3.1.50.

21 Basil of Caesarea, *On the Holy Spirit* 9.22. English translation from St. Basil the Great, *On the Holy Spirit*, trans. David Anderson, Popular Patristics Series (Crestwood, NY: St. Vladimir's Seminary Press, 1980).

22 Peter Lemesurier, *The Unknown Nostradamus: 500th Anniversary Biography* (London: John Hunt Publishing, 2003).

23 *On First Principles* 1.2.2. English translation from Origen, *On First Principles* vol. 1., ed. and trans. John Behr, Oxford Early Christian Texts (Oxford: Oxford University Press, 2017). We could say here that the Son has always been the "embodiment" of God's wisdom, but he of course was not technically embodied until the incarnation.

24 See, for example, the discussion in Larry W. Hurtado, *Lord Jesus Christ: Devotion to Jesus in Earliest Christianity* (Grand Rapids: Eerdmans, 2003), 114.

25 Athanasius of Alexandria, *On the Incarnation* 16. English translation from Saint Athanasius, *On the Incarnation*, trans. John Behr, Popular Patristics Series (Yonkers, NY: St. Vladimir's Seminary Press, 2011).

26 David E. Garland, *2 Corinthians*, Christian Standard Commentary (Nashville: Holman, 2021), 203–4.

27 See, for example, Athanasius of Alexandria, *Against the Arians* 1.14–15.

28 R. B. Jamieson, *The Paradox of Sonship: Christology in the Epistle to the Hebrews*, Studies in Christian Doctrine and Scripture (Downers Grove, IL: IVP Academic, 2021), 52, argues convincingly that the author of Hebrews makes a "sweeping movement from exaltation to eternal existence and back."

29 The author cites the Greek translation of the Hebrew Scriptures here.

30 For a thorough deep-dive on Trinitarian discourse in Hebrews, see Madison N. Pierce, *Divine Discourse in the Epistle to the Hebrews: The Recontextualization of Spoken Quotations of Scripture*, Society for New Testament Studies 178 (Cambridge: Cambridge University Press, 2020).

31 For example, James D. G. Dunn, *Did the First Christians Worship Jesus? The New Testament Evidence* (Louisville: Westminster John Knox, 2010), 130–32, in which he says that Jesus's "deity is unqualified" and "should not be played down."

32 *Against Heresies* 1.8.1. This unifying principle for Scripture falls under "the rule of faith," a shared assumption throughout much of the Christian tradition that Scripture is inspired by the triune God and thus is a noncontradictory, unified witness to him.

Scripture Index

OLD TESTAMENT

Genesis

1 .... 34, 37, 48, 136, 149
1:1–2 62
1:1–3 .... 6, 32
1:2 .... 111, 116
1:26–28 22
2:7 36
3:8 .... 116, 127
16:7–14 137
25:19–34   124
35:23 124

Exodus

3:11–15 52
3:14 .... 22, 131, 149
13 116
20:2–3 149
20:3 90
25–31 116
32 14

32–34 100
33:12–23 125
33:18–21 101
35–40 116

Leviticus

19:33–34 .... 72, 77

Numbers

23:19 97

Deuteronomy

6:4 .... 3, 7, 90, 92
6:16 2
32:43 140

Joshua

1:1 136

Judges

3:10 116

6:11–23 137

1 Samuel

16:13 116

2 Samuel

7:14 140

1 Kings

8 116
18 .... 91, 93
18:20–40 32

1 Chronicles

17:13 140

Nehemiah

9:5–6 44
9:6 36

Job

10:12 36

Psalm

2:4 33
2:7 140
3:8 .... 14, 106
33:11 35
36:9 36
37:13 33
45:6–7 140–41
89:13 127
89:27 124
91 2
97:7 140
102:25–27 41
110 6
110:1 141–42
115:1–8 32–33
116:2 127
121:4 63

Proverbs

15:3 153

Isaiah

6:1–3 146
6:3 85
11:2 153
11:2–3 82
42:8 38
40 17
40:8 85
43:19 17
43:25 14
44:22 17
55:11 136
63:10–14 62
65:17 14

Jeremiah

17:10 16
23:24 116
31 97–98

31:31–34 ....
96

Ezekiel

1:26–28   146–47
3:12 151
11:24 151
12:25 136–37

Joel

2:28 .... 6, 111
2:28-29 62

Micah

7:8 37

Haggai

2:5 63

Zechariah

4:6–10 152

Malachi

3:6 35

NEW TESTAMENT

Matthew

1:18 111
1:18–25 .... 172n9
3:1, 3 17
3:13–17   73, 111
3:14 24
3:16–17 23
4:1 111
4:1–11 2
6:10 125

9:1–8 13–19
9:8 46
12:8 45
12:18 112
13:17 17
16:15 40
26:29 125
28:17 93
28:18–20 21–28

Mark

1:2–5 17
3:28–30 .... 18, 57

Luke

3:2–6 17
22:20 97
24 .... 158–59, 161
24:27 .... 99, 158
24:32 158

24:44 .... 6, 138
24:44–45 159
24:49 26

John

1 .... 34–35, 44
1:1 6
1:1–3 ....54, 112
1:1–18 .... 23, 31–40
1:14 .... 5, 55
1:23 17
3:16 .... 4, 23
5................................. 75
5:17–30 43–49
5:24–27 54
5:26 54
5:38–40 98–99
5:44–47...............98–99
5:46......................... 6
8:49–51..................... 54
8:52–53 54
8:54–56 55
8:56........................... 17
8:57–58 56
8:58 51–58
8:59 57
10:18........................ 110
10:28–30 113
14–16 61–68
14:6 55
14:26 4
15:26 .... 4, 26
17:5............................. 26

Acts

1................................. 62
2 ....6–7, 62

Romans

7 73
8 71–78
8:29 129

1 Corinthians

1:24 64
2 160
2:1–5 83
2:1–16................... 81–87
2:8, 10–11..................84
2:16 85
8:4............................. 91
8:5–6a..................... 91
8:6b 91
8:6 89–93
8:14 85
13:12 .... 6, 36
15 .... 49, 120
15:20–23 130

2 Corinthians

1:20 19
3:1–18 95–102
3:3 97
3:4, 12 102
3:7–9 100
3:14–17 160
13:13 107
13:14..........................163

Galatians

1:1 48
2:20 77

Ephesians

1:1–14 105–13

1:2 106
1:3–6 109
1:3–14.........77, 124, 132
1:7–12 110
1:13–14 111

Philippians

2 45
2:5–11 ....115–21, 129
2:6 118
2:7–8 118–19
2:9–11 119–20

Colossians

1:16–17 128–29
1:15 .... 110, 125
1:15–20 .... 123–32, 138
1:17 54
1:18 129

2 Timothy

3:15–17 161
3:16–17........ 87, 96, 132

Hebrews

1:1 137
1:1–14 135–43
1:2a...........................138
1:3b...........................139
1:4 139
1:13 6
1:14.......................... 142
4:14–16 139
12:2....................93, 110
13:8........................... 97

1 Peter

1:1b–2 107
2:11 76
3:19 48

2 Peter

1:21 .... 143, 151

Revelation

1:4–5 145–54
1:8 150
1:10 151
1:11 151
2–3 150
2:8 150
4:1–2 150
4:2 151
4:8 151
4:11 26
5:6 152
17:3 151
19–22 48
21:10 151
21–22 .... 72, 124, 145
22:5 37
22:13 150

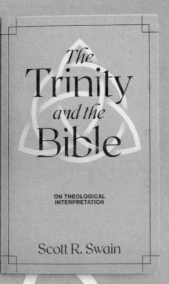